RECONSIDERING THE BICYCLE

In cities throughout the world, bicycles have gained a high profile in recent years, with politicians and activists promoting initiatives such as bike lanes, bikeways, bike-share programs, and other social programs to get more people on bicycles. Bicycles in the city are, some would say, the wave of the future for car-choked, financially-strapped, obese, and sustainability-sensitive urban areas.

This book explores how and why people are reconsidering the bicycle, no longer thinking of it simply as a toy or exercise machine, but as a potential solution to a number of contemporary problems. It focuses in particular on what reconsidering the bicycle might mean for everyday practices and politics of urban mobility, a concept that refers to the intertwined physical, technological, social, and experiential dimensions of human movement.

This book is for Introductory Anthropology, Cultural Anthropology, Cultural Sociology, Environmental Anthropology, and Urban Sociology courses.

Luis A. Vivanco is Associate Professor of Anthropology and Director of the Global and Regional Studies Program at the University of Vermont.

The Routledge Series for Creative Teaching and Learning in Anthropology
Editor: Richard H. Robbins, SUNY Plattsburgh

This series is dedicated to innovative, unconventional ways to connect undergraduate students and their lived concerns about our social world to the power of social science ideas and evidence. Our goal is to help spark social science imaginations and, in doing so, open new avenues for meaningful thought and action.

Available

Re-Imagining Milk by Andrea S. Wiley
Coffee Culture by Catherine M. Tucker
Lycra: How a Fabric Shaped America by Kaori O'Connor
Fake Stuff: China and the Rise of Counterfeit Goods by Yi-Chieh Jessica Lin
The World of Wal-Mart: Discounting the American Dream by Nicholas Copeland and Christine Labuski
Reading the iPod as an Anthropological Artifact by Lane DeNicola
Bicycles in the City: An Anthropological Perspective on a New (Old) Thing by Luis Vivanco
Alcohol: Social Drinking in Cultural Context by Janet Chrzan

Forthcoming

Trash by Monica Smith
Branding Gandhi by Ritu Khanduri
T-shirts by Kaori O'Connor

RECONSIDERING THE BICYCLE

An Anthropological Perspective on a New (Old) Thing

Luis A. Vivanco

University of Vermont

Routledge
Taylor & Francis Group

NEW YORK AND LONDON

First published 2013
by Routledge
711 Third Avenue, New York, NY 10017

Simultaneously published in the UK
by Routledge
2 Park Square, Milton Park, Abingdon, Oxon OX14 4RN

Routledge is an imprint of the Taylor & Francis Group, an informa business

Library of Congress Cataloging in Publication Data
Vivanco, Luis Antonio, 1969–
    Reconsidering the bicycle : an anthropological perspective on a
    new (old) thing / Luis A. Vivanco.
        p. cm.
    Includes bibliographical references and index.
    1. Bicycles.   2. Cycling.   I. Title.
    GV1041.V58 2013
    796.6—dc23

                                                    2012034586

ISBN: 978-0-415-50388-4 (hbk)
ISBN: 978-0-415-50389-1 (pbk)
ISBN: 978-0-203-58453-8 (ebk)

Typeset in New Baskerville
by RefineCatch Limited, Bungay, Suffolk, UK

SUSTAINABLE
FORESTRY
INITIATIVE

Certified Sourcing
www.sfiprogram.org
SFI-00555
The SFI label applies to the text stock.

Printed and bound in the United States of America by
Walsworth Publishing Company, Marceline, MO.

For Peggy, Isabel, Felipe, and Camila, with Love and Gratitude

"That simple and efficient little machine represents everything I believe in: sustainable living, a cleaner earth, egalitarianism, and community."
—Susie Stephens, Prominent U.S. Bicycle Advocate, 1999

"The mounted cyclist is a different person."
—Paul Fournel, *Need for the Bike*, 2003: 132

CONTENTS

FIGURES

BOXES

SERIES FOREWORD

The premise of these short books on the anthropology of stuff is that stuff talks, that written into the biographies of everyday items of our lives—coffee, T-shirts, computers, iPods, flowers, drugs, coffee, bicycles and so forth—are the stories that make us who we are and that makes the world the way it is. From their beginnings, each item bears the signature of the people who extracted, manufactured, picked, caught, assembled, packaged, delivered, purchased and disposed of it. And in our modern market-driven societies, our lives are dominated by the pursuit of stuff.

Examining stuff is also an excellent way to teach and learn about what is exciting and insightful about anthropological and sociological ways of knowing. Students, as with virtually all of us, can relate to stuff, while, at the same time, discovering through these books that it can provide new and fascinating ways of looking at the world.

Stuff, or commodities and things are central, of course, to all societies, to one extent or another. Whether it is yams, necklaces, horses, cattle, or shells, the acquisition, accumulation and exchange of things is central to the identities and relationships that tie people together and drive their behavior. But never, before now, has the craving for stuff reached the level it has; and never before have so many people been trying to convince each other that acquiring more stuff is what they most want to do. As a consequence, the creation, consumption, and disposal of stuff now threatens the planet itself. Yet to stop or even slow down the manufacture and accumulation of stuff necessary for economic growth would threaten the viability of our economy, on which our society is built.

This raises various questions. For example, what impact does the compulsion to acquire stuff have on our economic, social, and political well-being, as well as on our environment? How do we come to believe that there are certain things that we must have? How do we come to value some commodities or form of commodities above others? How does stuff define who we are? How have we managed to create commodity chains that link peasant farmers in Colombia or gold miners in Angola to wealthy residents of New York or teenagers in

Nebraska? Who comes up with the ideas for stuff and how do they translate those ideas into things for people to buy? Why do we sometimes consume stuff that is not very good for us? These short books examine such questions, and more.

Luis Vivanco's *Reconsidering the Bicycle* begins with the notion that movement is essential to the human condition, and examines why we think it is somehow natural to get into an automobile when we want to go somewhere, while others walk, take a bus or subway, or ride a two-wheeled vehicle. What are, he asks, the cultural, historical, social and environmental factors that go the decision of how to move?

Vivanco illustrates, as well, how the decision on how to move changes people in important ways, that moving through space requires the development of distinctive skills, symbolic meanings, ideologies and moral dilemmas, and even tastes in food. The person on a bicycle is thus different from the person in an automobile or riding public transit. The bicycle is an identity transforming object.

Furthermore, suggests Vivanco, the bicycle raises questions about changing urban landscapes, social movements, and how people create and maintain social status and identity. The book confronts students with the challenge of developing sustainable and just societies. And more than anything, it highlights the importance of mobility, particularly in dense urban landscapes. *Reconsidering the Bicycle: An Anthropological Perspective on a New (Old) Thing* provides students with a fresh vision of the stuff that comprises their own culture, and will, no doubt, prompt many not already doing so to get on their bikes.

Richard Robbins
State University of New York, Plattsburgh

PREFACE

The Bicycle, a New (Old) Thing

Soon after he took office as Chicago's new mayor in early 2011, Rahm Emanuel made a major policy announcement on the subject of bicycles. Just months before as a candidate, Emanuel, who had previously served as President Obama's Chief-of-Staff and as a Congressman, pledged that one of his main priorities as mayor would be to turn the Windy City into a "world-class bicycle city" in which using bicycles would become an integral part of Chicagoans' daily lives, "from kids on their first ride to senior citizens on their way to the grocery store" (Emanuel 2012). Now that he was mayor, Emanuel detailed his administration's plans to create 100 miles of protected bikeways—bike lanes separated from motorized vehicles by cones, curbs, or planters—by the time his term ends in 2015. He also described plans for the creation of a new $18 million bike-share program with 3,000 bicycles and 300 rental stations; a $75 million, 2.65 mile trail along Bloomingdale Avenue to accommodate bicycle commuters working Downtown and children getting to school; and a new ordinance that would require downtown buildings to provide protected storage facilities for bicycles. Since announcing these plans, the work has commenced in earnest: by Summer 2012, city workers put in several protected bike lanes, and a bike-share program opened with revised plans to be even bigger, with 5,000 bikes and 500 stations.

With its broad avenues and street grid, flat topography, and high density land-use patterns in which residential, work, and recreational opportunities lie close together, Chicago has a lot of potential to become an excellent bicycle city. It is already recognized widely for being pretty good, even with its harsh weather. Long before Mayor Emanuel's announcement, previous mayors had also had visions of Chicago as a bicycle city, from Harrison Carter II in 1897 who campaigned (and won) as "the cyclists' champion" during a time when bicycles were highly fashionable and Chicago was just becoming a hub of the American bicycle industry, to the "bicycling mayor" Richard M. Daley who, a century later, convened a bicycle advisory council and implemented the first real modern expansion of bicycle lanes, off-street recreational bike trails, and bicycle parking. Today Chicago has above-average rates of cycling for an American city (more than 1 percent of trips are by bicycle), numbers of cyclists have been growing fast, and in some areas bicycles are ubiquitous, such as along Milwaukee Avenue where 22 percent of the rush hour traffic is made up of people on bicycles (Lepeska 2011; Wisniewski 2011).

Mayor Emanuel's bicycle plan is nevertheless quite ambitious and it has provoked controversy and backlash. Some critics assert that it is irresponsible to focus on bicycles during a time when the city has a budget deficit of more than $640 million, 10 percent unemployment due to the economic recession, and a poverty rate of 1 out of 4 residents (Lepeska 2011). Others have raised moral concerns, identifying what they see as troubling patterns of elitism and even racism in Emanuel's plan, since many of the resources for bicycle infrastructure are going to be invested in the city's Downtown and affluent North Side, while lower income and minority neighborhoods have been slated to receive less. As one commentator noted, the focus on bicycles ". . . probably isn't going to help many low-income and out-of-work folks . . . You can't spend all your money on a single priority, ignoring transportation or anything else. Given the situation in Chicago, this much spending seems a bit out of whack" (quoted in Lepeska 2011). Furthermore, it's *bicycles*. In the car-centric world view that many Americans hold, Chicagoans among them, it's difficult to take the bicycle—that kids' toy, that sporting good, that thing that makes you sweat and work hard—seriously as a form of urban transportation.

It all begs the question, why would a new mayor with exceptional political credentials stake his administration's legitimacy on promoting the bicycle? The answer is not that Mayor Emanuel is a bicycle enthusiast (although apparently he is). It is much more about making changes in how the city functions in one of its most mundane dimensions—how people get around. Big problems stem from Chicago's over-stressed transportation system. The city's avenues and streets are often clogged with cars, motorists spend a lot of time stuck in traffic, and city work crews spend a lot of time repairing those roads. The city has high levels of automobile-related air pollution, which contribute to respiratory problems and asthma for more than 650,000 people in the metropolitan area. The city also has a 20 percent rate of childhood obesity and 60 percent of its adult residents are overweight or clinically obese, conditions that are closely tied to inactive lifestyles (City of Chicago 2005). As Mayor Emanuel has expressed, bicycling offers "a fast, fun, healthy, and affordable way to get around the city. In addition to providing a convenient alternative to driving, cycling reduces traffic congestion, promotes a cleaner environment, creates healthier communities, and improves the quality of life in our neighborhoods" (Emanuel 2012). But there is a fiscal dimension here too: all those transportation and public health problems entail big costs for the city, so finding a way to reduce costs by getting some people on bicycles is seen as a fiscally prudent strategy that could save millions of dollars.

It's also about economic competitiveness. Chicago competes on a global scale with other large post-industrial cities, such as New York, Los Angeles, San Francisco, London, Shanghai, and Paris, to attract capital investment, highly-educated service workers, and tourist dollars. These days one of the ways to do these things is to implement urban redevelopment initiatives to enhance "liveability," such as rezoning to promote high-end construction, developing entertainment and pedestrian districts, encouraging luxury consumption markets (such as artisanal food), and creating recreational spaces (Stein 2011). Liveability strategies often focus on limiting the noise, pollution, and congestion of automobiles and trucks, and emphasize the expansion of cost-effective and environmentally-friendly transportation alternatives such as improved mass rapid transit and greater use of bicycles. As President of the League of American Bicyclists, Andy Clarke, observed, promoting bicycles ". . . is what cities of the future are doing to attract businesses and young people. People don't want to drive all the time; they want a choice" (Walljasper 2012). Because these liveability initiatives are often targeted to appeal to middle and upper-class professionals, bicycles, not surprisingly, can develop a close symbolic association with gentrification and exacerbate social conflict in neighborhoods where class and racial differences are already tense.

Before going any further, I need to be clear that this book is not about Chicago, nor does it spend much time discussing politicians like Emanuel. This book is about bicycles. It explores how and why people are reconsidering the bicycle, no longer thinking of it simply as a toy or exercise machine, but as a potential solution to a number of contemporary problems. It focuses in particular on what reconsidering the bicycle might mean for everyday practices and politics of urban mobility, a concept that refers to the intertwined physical, technological, social, and experiential dimensions of human movement. It is still too early to know whether Mayor Emanuel's policy changes will make much of a difference for Chicago, if bicycles will become an integral part of life, or what the actual experience of riding in the city will be like in a few years. What makes Chicago worthy of mention here is partly its timeliness, as well as the fact that it is a large and high-profile city, so the sheer scale of what is being proposed justifiably turns heads. But also striking is the simple fact that there is something *common*—in the sense of ordinary and shared—at this historical moment in what Mayor Emanuel and his administration are trying to do. The fact is, in numerous cities throughout the U.S., as well as in the other cities of the Americas, Europe, Asia, and Africa, bicycles have gained a high profile in recent years, with politicians and activists promoting initiatives like bike lanes, bikeways, bike-share programs, and other social programs to get more people on bicycles. Bicycles in the city are, some would say, the wave of the future for car-choked, financially-strapped, obese, and sustainability-sensitive urban areas, and something for which Americans—60 percent of whom say they would bike more if conditions on roads were safer—may be ready (Walljasper 2012). As one San Francisco municipal transportation official recently remarked while visiting Chicago for a conference on cycling in cities, "Our preliminary analysis has shown us that bicycling will have the greatest growth [as a form of urban transportation], because it's such a great opportunity for the lowest cost in the shortest time frame" (Forbes 2012).

If bicycles are "the new thing," re-envisioned as a transformative vehicle at the cutting edge of urban change, it has to be said that they are a new *old* thing. Bicycles have been around for over a century and have enjoyed periods of fashionable popularity and a reputation for being involved at the cutting edge of social change, in the 1890s, for example. As this book will show, there are important contours to how and why bicycles have become desirable and useful in different places and at different times, contours that are closely tied to complex and dynamic interplays of technological innovation, industrial capitalism, consumerism, advocacy movements, urban change, and national and cultural particularities. Equally important here is the idea that bicycles are "things" in the sense that as machines they are actual material objects—not just ciphers onto which specific groups of people project their own desires and uses—and the very materiality of the machine contributes to the experience and perceptions of its users. Further, as material objects, bicycles are not static or unidimensional things, factors that make those experiences and perceptions all the more interesting.

That bicycles offer a solution to complex urban problems, that their presence in cities supports more liveable urban spaces, or that they offer a "fast, fun, healthy and affordable way to get around the city" (as Mayor Emanuel says) are not self-evident facts. These ideas about bicycles are meaningful within specific historical and social conditions, and they provoke controversy precisely because they run against the grain of current thinking in specific urban contexts and political arenas, or because particular social and material conditions on the ground suggest something completely different. Often these things have little to do directly with bicycles themselves, and so a focus on urban bicycle mobility offers a useful lens through which we can examine a range of issues, such as current dilemmas of health, sustainability, and globalization confronting urban dwellers and politics. But on close inspection, it turns out that there is also very little that is self-evident about bicycles themselves. Central to the anthropological approach I take here is the idea that bicycles are heterogeneous, multidimensional, and contextual objects, enmeshed in specific technological conditions, practices of life, social relations, cultural meanings, and political-economic dynamics. One of the central conclusions is that these conditions help produce important variations across cities, countries, and social groups in how people think about and interact with bicycles in their everyday lives.

ACKNOWLEDGMENTS

The decision to write a book is never a wholly individual one. It emerges out of social relationships, relies heavily on them to get the thing done, and, in some cases, impacts them profoundly, which one always hopes will be for the better. The seeds of this particular book emerged out of a conversation with my friend and colleague, Richard Watts, whose devilishly modest question "have you ever thought about doing research on bicycles and transportation?," when it actually sank in several weeks later, sent me hurtling off on a new intellectual journey when I decided to try to figure out what a cultural anthropologist who uses a bicycle for everyday transportation and enjoys long bike rides might have to say about the subject. Thanks are due to Richard for helping me get my initial footing in the field of transportation research, and for traveling with me for long stretches as this and other projects on bicycles have unfolded.

This book has benefited from the support of two interdisciplinary programs at the University of Vermont, the Global and Regional Studies Program and the Transportation Research Center, that have both provided financial support for this project, including funding to travel to the Transportation Research Board annual meeting and development funds for a course on the Anthropology of Mobility from which some of the ideas in this book emerge. I am especially grateful to the TRC, where I have been received with generosity and collegiality by faculty, researchers, staff, and graduate students, among them Lisa Aultman-Hall, Jim Sullivan, Glenn McRae, Austin Troy, and especially Brian Lee, who graciously allowed me to sit in on his bicycle planning course during Spring 2011. My perspectives on the intersections between bicycling and transportation have been deeply enriched as well by my ongoing research collaborations with Stephanie Kaza, Josh Farley, and Phoebe Spencer.

I also want to thank my colleagues and students in Anthropology at UVM who have helped me think through the relationship between culture and bicycles. Rob Gordon, Ben Eastman, and Scott Van Kueren have been especially engaged and supportive with useful feedback and suggestions. Rob Welsch has made extraordinary contributions to this book, by listening, asking good questions, and providing sound advice about theoretical and ethnographic matters at every turn. The opportunities to teach the courses "Bicycles, Globalization, and Sustainability" and "Anthropology of Mobility" have contributed immeasurably to my thinking about bicycles, and I want to thank the students in these courses who've contributed their energy, questions, and insights.

My thanks extend as well to those in the "bike world" with whom I've grown close in recent years, who have been supportive of this project and helped shape it in various ways. I especially want to thank Phil Hammerslough, Stu Lindsay, Chapin Spencer, Jason Van Driesche, Jon Adams-Kolitz, Glenn Eames, Hubert D'Autremont, Jeremy Grandstaff, Andy Crawford, and Christine Hill. Thanks to Lisa Russo, who has an uncanny ability to send something bike-related at opportune moments. And special thanks to Josh Brown who made an important contribution to this project as it was nearing completion that helped me maintain my sanity and sense of purpose.

I also want to thank Richard Robbins, series editor, who has not only inspired me as a teacher and scholar throughout my career, but encouraged me to frame my work on bicycles through the lens of everyday stuff. At Routledge, Stephen Rutter has shown great patience and contributed his own useful ideas to this project. Sam Barbaro has provided useful assistance at well. The three reviewers, Catherine Lutz, Brown University; Giselinde Kuipers, University of Amsterdam; and Michael Carolan, Colorado State University, have each offered highly useful feedback.

Most of all, I want to thank my family for their support. My parents, Ed and Diane, have provided encouragement for my interest in bicycles since I was little, and it continues today. I am especially grateful to my wife Peggy, and kids Isabel, Felipe, and Camila, for their shared commitment to this project. In particular, Peggy's sacrifices to make this project a reality are as much as my own, and without her none of this would have happened. Writing a book is a whole family commitment. My family's willingness to put up with all my bicycle talk and days of writing is only a part of it; it is their encouragement (and cajoling near the end) that has made all difference. This book is dedicated to them.

1

ANTHROPOLOGY, BICYCLES, AND URBAN MOBILITY

"Whoever thought it would come to this? Our cavalcade grows exponentially! Hath you seen it? On the roadways of every city there are bicyclists emerging again after a century in shadows. We are here to claim what's rightfully ours: respectful free movement on streets everywhere. In Milwaukee, and Pittsburgh, Dallas, too, and Bellingham, Grand Rapids, and Los Angeles, even!"

—*Boneshaker*, bicycle 'zine, 2011

During the Fall of 2011, General Motors, the largest automobile company in the world, began running an advertisement targeted at U.S. college students. The ad, which appeared in posters placed around college campuses and in campus newspapers throughout the country, shows an image of a young man wearing a backpack sitting on a bicycle, shielding his embarrassed face with one of his hands, while an attractive young woman smiles at him from a car. Splashed across the top of the ad, in bold print, it says, "REALITY SUCKS. Luckily the GM college discount doesn't." With the tag line "Stop Pedaling . . . Start Driving," the ad explains that college students and recent graduates are eligible to receive a special discount of anywhere from several hundred to several thousand dollars on a new GM car or truck.

That such an ad exists is not especially remarkable. Automobile ads are ubiquitous in our public sphere, tailored carefully to appeal to specific audiences with special messages and incentives. This particular ad communicates a (possibly amusing) message that a lot of American college students can probably relate to: having been driven around in cars since they were little, and then driving themselves in their teenage years, they are reduced to *riding bicycles*, an inferior and undignified state of affairs, because money is tight or maybe because their college limits the number of cars on campus. But it's a temporary thing. Because bicycles are children's toys, and adults who ride them are not quite grown up, or worse, they wear *lycra shorts*. Because automobiles are cool, innovative, and fast, and bicycles are not. And because bicycling is an impractical, inconvenient, maybe even dangerous way to get around. Once you return to the "real world" beyond college, the ad communicates, you can get on with your life, a life in which the automobile plays an obvious and central role.

These ideas about cars and bicycles are familiar to many Americans. But what *is* remarkable in this situation is that not long after the ads appeared, there was a public outpouring of rage and resentment from cyclists, many of them people who use bicycles as their primary means of getting around. Across the internet—in blogs, online forums, Twitter feeds, and viral emails—thousands of them laid into GM and its top executives for spreading an anti-bicycle message. National bicycle advocacy groups based in Washington, D.C., and their allies in dozens of cities and towns throughout the country, alerted their members to write letters and send emails of complaint to GM. The world's largest bicycle company, Taiwan-based Giant Bicycles, even remade the original GM ad using an image of gridlocked traffic, and a message "REALITY **DOES** SUCK. Luckily bicycles don't . . .". With its own tag line of "Stop driving . . . start pedaling," Giant's ad declares that cycling is healthy at any age and, compared with the massive expenditures associated with buying and maintaining an automobile, can save you thousands of dollars a year. Facing this unexpected backlash (and recognizing that among the 57 million Americans who ride bicycles are a lot of car owners), GM pulled its ads, expressed regret for any disrespect it may have communicated to cyclists, and promised to change its campaign's message.

Reflecting on the situation not long after GM pulled the ad, one blogger observed, "When a car company publicly apologizes—multiple times—for making an anti-bike ad *and* promises to change it? Could you have seen that happening five years ago? I think we're getting somewhere."

Reconsidering the Bicycle

It is difficult to tell where that "somewhere" is, but the bicycle does seem to be enjoying what a pair of transportation planners recently termed a "renaissance" (Pucher et al. 2011) and one journalist even called a "pedaling revolution" (Mapes 2009). Not only is the bicycle industry enjoying booming sales, in dozens of major cities and hundreds of suburbs throughout the United States, among them the country's most important urban centers—New York, Chicago, San Francisco, Minneapolis, Boston, Philadelphia, Boulder, Portland, Madison, Los Angeles, and Washington, D.C. to name a few—people have been taking to bicycles in noticeable, even surprising, numbers. The rise in cycling may not be quite "exponential" as the epigraph above expresses—it also tends to be gendered (with men constituting the majority of new riders)—but the number of bicycle trips made in the U.S. has been growing, much faster than the rate of population growth. Between 1977 and 2009, for example, the total number of bicycle trips has tripled, the pace of that increase intensifying during the past five years (Pucher et al. 2011). Much of that growth has been in urban areas where people have turned to using bicycles as a utilitarian vehicle, and where currently 52 percent of all bike trips are for practical purposes, the rest being for recreation or exercise (Pucher et al. 2011). In certain cities, rates of growth in cycling have been astonishing, such as a 77 percent increase in New York City in the past five years, and since 2007, 80 percent increase in Washington, D.C.

One of the most striking features of the bicycle's rise is that it involves an upheaval in meanings surrounding the object itself. Americans are accustomed to thinking of the bicycle as a child's toy or as a performance machine for the lycra-clad competitor or recreational enthusiast, but with its current rise there is a new sensitivity to the bicycle as a functional vehicle for getting around in everyday life. In the current zeitgeist, this shift in meanings can denote a couple of things. One is a growing recognition that bicycles can provide a useful, quick, healthy, inexpensive, technologically-simple, efficient, and even enjoyable method of getting from point A to B. This usefulness is especially true in flat and dense urban areas where the distances are relatively short, and where persistent traffic congestion makes it a pain to get around by car. The other idea here is more focused on the bicycle as a tool of socio-political, environmental, and cultural change. As the late Susie Stephens, a prominent bicycle advocate during the 1990s, expressed, the bicycle creates "sustainable living, a cleaner earth, egalitarianism, and community." In an era of public concern over increasingly expensive fossil fuels, global warming, the sustainability of consumption-oriented lifestyles, an obesity epidemic, and interest in reducing the scale of everyday life, the bicycle helps people "get around how they get around" (Figure 1.1). In other words, it appears to offer a viable, effective, and, perhaps above all, sustainable alternative to the transportation status quo, which in the U.S. revolves around the private automobile.

The rise of the bicycle in recent years is thus set against a backdrop of automobile dominance, what some scholars call a condition of "hyperauto-mobility" (Adams 2001; Freund and Martin 2007; Vannini 2009). The United States is, to an historically and globally unmatched extent, a nation of private automobile users. As the National Household Travel Survey (2009) shows, almost 90 percent of the "trips"—defined in transportation research circles as "mobility for a purpose"—that Americans make are by private automobile. Americans spend on average 18.5 hours a week in a car, typically driving about 40 miles per day. Some of that time is spent getting to and from work (91 percent of American workers drive in a car to work every day) but most of it (80 percent) is spent involved in the mundane activity of running errands—going to the grocery store, picking up the kids, dropping off the laundry. Half of all discrete trips Americans take are under three miles and 40 percent under two miles— both of which are generally considered "bikeable distance" for most adults— and yet still only about 1 percent of overall trips Americans take are by bicycle.

Figure 1.1 **Climate Action, San Francisco.**
Source: Universal Images Group Editorial

With more than 250 million registered automobiles, the highest number of any country on the planet, Americans are often told that they love their automobiles. It would be difficult to say otherwise to a NASCAR fan, a vintage car collector, or the automobile advertising executives who created the GM ad campaign discussed above. But for most Americans, love is not really the point. Automobiles are a fact of life, a taken-for-granted necessity for doing the things they expect, and are expected, to do in their lives. During the twentieth century the U.S. underwent unprecedented change as our economy, social relations, residential patterns, and landscape were reorganized around mass automobilization. Automobiles came to occupy the heart of American industrial and economic growth (reflected in the famous quotation "What's good for General Motors is good for the country"), how Americans think of themselves as a nation (as inventive people who love the speed, freedom, and technological progress associated with cars), and at least since the 1950s, where they live (in sprawling suburbs without public transportation where cars are necessary to get around). This transformation has been buttressed by a powerful "car ideology" that shapes how they view the world, structuring and limiting their most basic perceptions of how to get around, what to spend their money on, and what kinds of risks they accept (Lutz and Fernandez 2010: 11).

Yet even as it seems difficult, undesirable, or downright traitorous to imagine an alternative to the automobile, this condition of hyperautomobility exerts a heavy toll: *On American lives and bodies,* with 35,000 to 40,000 deaths and 2 million injuries each year due to collisions (Lutz and Fernandez 2010); long-term chronic issues related to the carcinogenic substances people breathe from automobile emissions (Deka 2004); and a public health crisis in which lack of physical activity is a major cause of high rates of obesity (Pucher et al. 2010). *On economic productivity,* in which American businesses lose six billion person hours and over $100 billion in productivity each year due to traffic congestion (Federal Highway Administration 2011). *On personal income,* in which the average expenditure to keep a car running is $8,000 per year, and over a lifetime of driving an average expenditure of about $1 million per household is spent on cars and their upkeep (Lutz and Fernandez 2010). *On social relations,* in which automobility fosters individuality, competition, rejection of collective responsibility, aggressiveness, and domination by way of movement, speed, and escape (Bauman 2000: 12). *On social equality,* in which social groups that have less access to cars, or choose not to use them, including the elderly, poor, youth, disabled, non-car owners, and members of immigrant groups and ethnic minorities, are endangered or experience inhibited mobility because of automobile domination (Cass, Shove, and Urry 2005). *And on the environment,* in which automobiles consume 70 percent of the petroleum this country uses, emit critical amounts of greenhouse gases linked to climate change, and motivate the creation of extensive road networks and parking lots (enough to cover an area the size of Connecticut) that disrupt biodiversity and cause run-off of toxic substances into waterways (Bae 2004; Deka 2004; Lutz and Fernandez 2010).

Enter the bicycle. Or maybe *re*-enter the bicycle. Beginning back in the 1970s, a number of strong voices emerged clamoring for a change in our automobile dominant transportation system, arguing that it was leading toward a "carmageddon," in which the "energy slavery" of petroleum dependence was generating an impending ecological catastrophe, and bicycles offered a useful alternative (Illich 1977). A loosely organized "bike movement" formed, and its major accomplishment throughout the 1970s and 1980s was to gain for cyclists the legal right to ride as vehicles on the roads. Today, in an era of public concern over environmental sustainability and obesity, the bike movement has new legs, and has reemerged as a vocal and often effective lobbying presence in national and local government (Wray 2008; Mapes 2009). Cycling advocacy groups have been joined in their promotion of the bicycle by environmentalists, urban neighborhood activists, and even public health officials, all of whom have begun shifting their attention toward the realm of transportation policy and planning, based on a perception of the bicycle's key role in promoting non-polluting sustainable transportation, a locally-oriented lifestyle, quality of life, and community health (Batterbury 2003; Horton 2006; Parkin 2012). It is not uncommon in these circles to hear that the bicycle represents a simple solution to the many complex problems confronting contemporary society. As a Boston-based activist explained at a bicycle advocacy summit I attended, "If I were running for office, here is what my campaign platform would be. Less crime. Better school performance. Reduced greenhouse gases. Better looking communities. Friendlier neighborhoods. A more prosperous business district. And you know how I would be able to achieve these things? Bicycles. All we have to do is create the conditions to get people riding bicycles."

Politicians long beholden to the automobile are also rethinking the bicycle. One indication of this fact is the increase since the 1990s at the federal level of investment in bicycle-related infrastructure and programs, which has hovered between $600 million and $1 billion a year during the past several years. Although even $1 billion is a drop in the bucket compared to the more than $100–120 billion invested in automobile-related highway and road expenditures, bicycle advocates were further encouraged when Ray LaHood, U.S. Secretary of Transportation, announced in early 2010 "the end of favoring motorized transportation at the expense of non-motorized." Declaring it a "sea change" in federal policy, LaHood announced that the government would thereafter integrate the needs of cyclists in federally funded transportation projects, discourage transportation investments that negatively affect cyclists, and encourage investments that go beyond minimum requirements to meet the needs of cyclists and walkers. Explaining the decision, LaHood wrote in his blog (LaHood 2010), "Look, bike projects are relatively fast and inexpensive to build and are environmentally sustainable; they reduce travel costs; dramatically improve safety and public health; and reconnect citizens with their communities."

At the municipal level, many city leaders have also begun to think of the bicycle as a cost-effective way to address some pressing practical and political problems. These problems include persistent traffic congestion, populist backlashes against ill-conceived road projects, pressure to meet city targets for reductions in greenhouse gas emissions, preparations for a post-oil future, and demands to remain competitive with other cities that offer a high quality of life, which typically means public spaces devoid of noisy and polluting automobiles (Mapes 2009; Furness 2010). As a result, dozens of U.S. cities have been implementing bicycle-friendly projects, such as bike-share programs, bike lane expansions, and incentive and education programs to get more people bicycling. Such projects have not been uncontroversial, generating in some places, most notably New York City, "a simmering cultural conflict between competing notions of urban transportation" (Goodman 2010; Blickstein 2010). In the past couple of years, the city has seen a rise in sharp tensions and open conflicts between bicycle advocates and critics who complain ardently of inconsiderate cyclists, or the dedication of precious public funds toward the interests of a minority of users. When a well-known *Wall Street Journal* columnist joined in the fray—he wrote "A fibrosis of bicycle lanes is spreading through the cities of the world. The well-being of innocent motorists is threatened as traffic passageways are choked by the spread of dull whirs, sharp whistles, and sanctimonious pedal-pushing" (O'Rourke 2011)—it was clear that the city's pursuit of bicycle-friendliness was grating on some prominent nerves.

These efforts and their controversies do not exist in a global vaccuum, which is to say that bicycles are on agendas for urban social change across the world. Indeed, bicycle advocates in the U.S. explain why and how the American transportation system can accommodate the bicycle by pointing to non-U.S. examples of bicycle-friendly innovations. Amsterdam (The Netherlands), Copenhagen (Denmark), and Freiburg (Germany) are among the first to be mentioned, not simply because of their high rates of cycling (upwards of 30–40 percent of all trips are by bicycle in these cities), but because those high rates of cycling were achieved in spite of the fact that these countries, like the U.S., have histories of mass motorization. In London, Paris, Bogotá, Mexico City, Montreal, Vancouver, Barcelona, and Berlin (among many others), leaders have recently made high profile commitments to promoting bicycles, implementing bicycle-only avenues, charging cars to enter the city center, creating bike-share programs, and aggressively expanding bike lanes. And in Asian countries like China and Japan, the bicycle remains a common—and in some places, dominant—mode of urban mobility. Even as the growing middle classes of Beijing and Shanghai in China aspire to own automobiles, 20 percent of trips in those cities continue to be by bicycle; in other Chinese cities, rates of cycling remain much higher (Gardner 1998; Haixiao 2012). Delegations of mayors and urban planners from the U.S. have been traveling to and from some of these places, searching for inspiration and practical guidance on how to implement bicycle-friendly solutions back home.

The point of all this is not that there is a worldwide bicycle conspiracy, much less a tightly coordinated international effort to promote bicycles. If anything, even as bicycles outsell automobiles worldwide by a margin of almost two to one (130 million bicycles vs. 70 million automobiles produced in 2007; Brown 2010), transportation experts project a global future of increasing automobility, in which a current world total of 850 million automobiles could lead to upwards of 2 billion by 2050 as the U.S., European, and Asian automobile industries turn their attention to new frontiers of expansion in Chinese and Indian markets (Shafer and Victor 2000). Rather, the social and political energy coalescing around the bicycle as a utilitarian vehicle in particular seems be speaking to a number of widespread concerns and ambivalences in people's everyday lives, among them the environmental consequences of petroleum dependence—including global climate change and localized air pollution—as well as persistent traffic congestion, the disruptive effects of road projects and traffic on neighborhood cohensiveness and access to public goods, crises in public health associated with sedentary lifestyles, the financial and social costs of daily travel, and the negative quality of life impacts of automobiles.

The title phrase of Tour de France bicycle racer Lance Armstrong's 2001 autobiography—"It's not about the bike"—seems apt here, which is to say, the heart of the matter lies beyond the bike. Although what Armstrong is getting at (his drive to overcome cancer while pursuing a career as a professional cyclist) is different from the discussion about the bicycle's usefulness as a practical urban vehicle, the phrase implies that paying attention to bicycles might help us see other things, providing a lens through which to examine critical dilemmas confronting urban dwellers in the U.S. and globally.

Toward an Anthropology of Urban Bicycle Mobility

But what if we also take seriously the claims, expressed by the Boston-based bicycle advocate above, not to mention many cyclists themselves, of the bicycle's transformative potential as a means of getting around? In this view, it isn't a matter of simply looking "beyond the bike," because the bicycle itself—the actual material object—is credited as a cause of social and individual transformation. In other words, maybe it *is* about the bike, perhaps there *is* something important about what the bike itself does for and with people, a perspective that highlights the technological underpinnings of the bicycle's recent rise.

One of the main tasks of this book is to convey the cultural, historical, and political-economic conditions under which such claims about bicycles might be meaningful. Bicycles are heterogeneous and contextual objects that are used for many reasons, especially for sport and recreation, but my specific goal here is to develop an anthropological perspective on bicycles and their role in urban mobility, "mobility" here referring to the intertwined physical, technological, social, and experiential dimensions of human movement. Based on ethnographic research in my own city and analyses of selective urban settings around the globe, it pays careful attention to the bicycle as a material object, the social worlds and experiences of those who use it and advocate for its use in everyday urban mobility, and the analytical potential of using the bicycle as a lens into contemporary dilemmas of urban life, sustainability, social change, and globalization. Bicycles are also quintessentially globalized commodities; they are not only ridden in pretty much all corners of the world but their production from raw materials to finished product involves economic, social, and political relationships between many countries. As a result, in order to develop a holistic understanding of the bicycle requires an understanding of the bicycle's histories and transnational contexts of development, manufacture, marketing, and retail, because these dynamics also shape the kinds of social relationships that are possible with bicycles.

One of the practical problems facing me as a cultural anthropologist is that my discipline has not, in fact, taken the bicycle seriously, producing a pittance of studies on bicycles and their cultures (Gilley 2006; Jirón 2009; Fowler 2011). Nevertheless, as this book and the series in which it appears aim to demonstrate, anthropology *is* good at thinking about stuff, the everyday objects and goods in our lives. One of the interesting things about stuff, notes Daniel Miller (2010: 155), is its "capacity for fading from view, and becoming naturalized, taken for granted, the background or frame to our behavior" even as it guides and influences human behavior. Bringing bicycles into view allows us consider the influences of stuff on peoples' lives, and it raises a number of key issues and dilemmas that a lot of people (including anthropologists) are thinking about these days: the rapid movement of people, goods, and ideas across borders; the causes and consequences of contemporary consumption patterns; changing urban landscapes and cultures; the ability of social movements to effect political change; how people create and manage social status and identity; and the challenge of developing sustainable and just societies. Bicycles touch on all these issues, and the purchase or riding of a bicycle are more than practical choices: bicycling has important economic, political, social, and cultural dimensions that endow certain kinds of meanings on the object and its user, meanings that vary across social groups and cultures (Ebert 2004).

The low profile of bicycles within anthropology might be explained by observing that, generally-speaking, bicycle research is itself a small and marginal area of scholarship. A handful of bicycle scholars are located at the fringes of historical and sociological studies of technology, leisure, or sport (i.e., Pivato 1990; Bjiker 1995; Rosen 2002; Mackintosh and Norcliffe 2007; Horton 2006; Cox 2008), but most (still a handful, relatively speaking) are situated in the interdisciplinary field of transportation research, which is dominated by engineers and urban planners. The widespread symbolism of bicycles as kid's toys or sporting goods is at least partially responsible for this state of affairs, which makes it more difficult to take them seriously as a site of technological innovation or as a viable form of transportation. Furthermore, reflecting a hierarchical logic embedded in Americans' contemporary travel patterns, a lot of the research in transportation studies focuses on automobiles and to a lesser degree planes, ships, and trains. The orientation within the transportation research field is mostly practical, with researchers tending to focus on engineering and planning problems like identifying the most appropriate materials for road construction under certain climatic or user conditions; how to use new technologies for regulating traffic flow in transportation corridors; or what policies and driver education programs work best to improve highway safety. Most research on bicycles reflects a similar practical orientation, but one indication of its marginality within the transportation research field is that bicycles are combined with pedestrian issues, an area typically referred to in shorthand as "bike-ped" even as most transportation experts (not to mention cyclists and walkers) recognize crucial differences between the needs of each.

During the twentieth century, keeping people and goods moving in an efficient, rapid, cost-effective, and safe manner became a central political and economic priority in the U.S. and other industrialized countries. Transportation research in support of these goals is thus of great importance. Yet anthropology has largely been absent within the field. Indeed, in 2010 when I attended the annual meeting of the Transportation Research Board—the most important conference of the transportation research world with some 11,000 transportation officials and researchers in attendance—not a single anthropologist presented any research, and I suspect I was the only anthropologist there. Surprising, perhaps, especially since appreciating the diverse ways human movement and travel are structured and experienced is of inherent interest to our discipline (Ingold 2011). Not only that; in recent decades, anthropology has shifted from being a discipline interested primarily in studying "roots"— localized communities rooted in particular places—to one that is also interested in "routes," that is, the movement and circulation of people, objects, and social relationships (Appadurai 1996; Clifford 1997).

I think one possible reason anthropology is largely absent in mainstream transportation research—which also extends to bicycle scholarship—may have something to do with the latter's tendency to frame transportation issues around practical and engineering questions at the expense of basic sociocultural questions about the social dimensions and tacit meanings people make about their experiences of getting around in their everyday lives. Anthropologists are interested in the social patterns and dynamics that shape what a certain group of people take for granted as the natural, inevitable, or right way of doing things, as well as the social relationships, institutions, meanings, and collective behaviors that uphold that particular way of thinking and acting. As a result, anthropologists might ask: Why is it "natural" that when many Americans need to go somewhere, they get in a car, while for others it might be on foot, a bus, subway, or a two-wheeled vehicle? What social, ideological, historical, environmental, and institutional factors and norms shape a decision to drive, walk, or ride, or, alternatively, prevent people from doing any one of these things? How might these same factors pattern how people actually perceive, experience, and practice these things in their everyday lives? What are the consequences of moving around in the ways people do, on their physical bodies, social identities, perceptions of themselves and the places they live, ideas about what is right or wrong, notions of space and time, and the way their communities are socially and spatially organized? In addressing these kinds of questions, anthropology's goal is not to deliberately skirt pragmatic concerns, but to provide a deeper level of insight into the social organization and cultural meanings of mobility practices and the objects involved in them, demonstrating that what may feel "natural" is the product of social and cultural processes that vary across time and space and may not always be visible to everyone involved.

I also think there is a basic conceptual limitation with the term "transportation" that prevents deeper engagement with the fullness of these social and cultural processes. Transportation is generally defined as an act of carrying or conveying something or someone, which tends to place an emphasis on the means or the system of conveyance itself rather than the people involved. Unwittingly or not, "transportation" imagines people as objects, or "passengers," to be moved, which these days implies to be moved within in a system of mass movement and travel organized along industrial principles of speed and efficiency (Illich 1977; Sachs 1992). Often missing here are actual people, people as living, breathing beings whose willingness and ability to move are enabled and constrained by both material and cultural factors, among them what technological aids to travel exist, individual choices and preferences, perceptions of time and distance, social norms and expectations, and the embodied demands and experiences of the movement itself.

Why does all of this matter for a study on bicycles? Pointing out the conceptual limitations of the term "transportation" may feel a bit like splitting hairs. But in order to develop an anthropological approach to bicycles and bicycle mobility, it is necessary to take seriously what bicycles do to, for, and with people as well as what people do with them, not simply how they might be practically integrated into a transportation system (although as an everyday bicycle rider, I am deeply sympathetic with the transportation research scholars struggling with this problem). Of course, in some senses bicycles do actually convey people. But people are also actively involved in powering and directing bicycles, a dynamic reflected in John Howard's famous observation, "The bicycle is a curious vehicle. Its passenger is its engine." The result is a relationship, even a temporal fusion or assemblage, between human and machine that is distinctive from other vehicles in what it requires, enables, and effects. Wind rushing through one's hair, legs pulsating, feelings of vulnerability and fear mixed with exhilaration, a special knowledge of the spatial layout of one's neighborhood— it is not difficult to recognize how riding a bicycle has experiential, sensual, and social repercussions on one's life that are different from driving a car, riding on a train, or walking as a pedestrian. In other words, bicycles, like all technologies, extend human bodies and capabilities, but they extend our bodies and capabilities in specific ways. The resulting relationship between human and machine is distinctive from any other, enabling and requiring certain things of peoples' bodies and opening them up to certain kinds of interactions with their environments. Furthermore, even within the same society, individuals approach and experience bicycles in different ways, according to gender, age, class, and ethnicity (Horton et al. 2007).

The broader issue here is that a critical understanding of mobility in everyday life begins with recognizing that there are diverse modes, technologies, skills, and infrastructures related to movement (Ingold 2004; Jensen 2009: xvii) (see Box 1.1). As one scholar observes, ". . . means of transportation are not mere conduits of space. Ships, buses, bicycles, yachts, trains, and training spaceship stations are the contexts of unique performances, dramas, experiences, and interactions" (Vannini 2009: 11). In each of these contexts, the kind of movement possible (fast or slow, tracked or untracked, open or closed to the elements, collective or individual, etc.) is shaped by the technology involved as well as the environment in which it takes place, not to mention the physical and social infrastructure (roads, streets, ports, laws, regulations, institutions, etc.) and skill sets necessary to facilitate that movement (Pelzer 2010).

Different mobilities carry the potential for knowing, sensing, and interacting with the world in specific ways, and are closely associated with certain practices of life. Put simply, if a bicycle is your main mode of getting around, you are likely to know and interact with the city differently than if you regularly ride on a bus or drive a car. In all cases, scholars observe that distinctive mobilities are associated with informal and "distinctive forms of . . . life, each with characteristic rhythms, concerns, and social interactions" (Patton 2005). Reinforcing this point, mobilities scholar John Urry (2007) asserts that "different mobilities constitute different kinds of society." By this he means that how people move is not just patterned by culture and social relations—a point I've tried to make clear above—but also generates new and distinctive social relationships, identities, and local cultures. In other words, people create local social relations and cultures of mobility based on norms and conventions specific to that place. As a result, as I will discuss in a later chapter, the everyday use of the bicycle in Amsterdam, the Netherlands, takes place in a local mobility culture distinct from the northeastern U.S. streets on which I ride daily. The informal codes,

Box 1.1 Understanding Mobility

Mobility is not just movement through geographic space. It is culturally meaningful and socially, economically, and a politically organized movement involving changes in social condition or status. It is possible to move and not be mobile (think of getting up from a couch to go to the bathroom), just as it is possible to be mobile without moving (think about sitting in your room while surfing the internet or talking on a cell phone). A useful way to think about mobility is the following (adapted from Urry 2007):

Mobility is a change of condition that has three interdependent dimensions—movements, networks, and motility—in which:

Movements involve the circulation in and through physical and/ or social space.

Networks are those frameworks and infrastructure, themselves often immobile, that enable and limit mobility.

Motility is the capacity an actor has to move or be mobile.

Opportunities for Reflection and Action

To better understand how this concept of mobility relates to bicycles, make a list of the specific movements, networks, and motilities involved in riding a bicycle. What are the specific dimensions of bicycle mobility? What are the changes in condition involved in riding a bicycle? How do the qualities of movement, networks, and motility involved in riding a bicycle differ from those involved in driving a car, walking, or riding in an airplane?

rules, skills, and embodied practices appropriate to riding in each setting differ. To appreciate these differences, it is necessary to move beyond the common perception of mobility as unproductive and wasted time—the seemingly "empty" moments while moving from point A to B—and begin to recognize that mobility is itself a location of meaning making, identity formation, and cultural production in localized settings (Creswell 2006; Jensen 2009; Vannini 2009; Ingold 2011).

These days most anthropologists take for granted that people create and recreate culture all the time, from the most dramatic human settings—revolutions and warfare, for example—to the most mundane, like cooking a meal, waiting for a subway, or riding a bicycle (Ehn and Löfgren 2010). We also recognize that the (re)creation of culture is a contested process involving politics, power, and social inequality. Placed in a mobilities context, it means that how people move around presupposes and generates social competition and struggle, not just on the streets themselves but in city halls and other settings where political decision-making takes place regarding mobility. Further, although Americans like to believe they are free to move around however they want to, Creswell (2001: 19) observes that "free and equal mobility is a deception." Part of the reason for this lack of freedom is that different social groups have different relationships to a given form of mobility: some are more in charge of it than others; some initiate flows and others do not; some are more on the receiving end of it than others; and some are excluded or even imprisoned by it (Massey 1993: 61). Another reason is that specific forms of mobility are accorded differing levels of symbolic prestige, economic investment, and political support based on what position they occupy in a hierarchically-arranged system of mobility. To many urban cyclists in the U.S. right now, these may not be such surprising revelations; indeed, they daily experience a kind of social marginality as they are literally yelled at, or pushed to the sides of roads and onto sidewalks by more dominant automobiles, or, for that matter, experience advertising campaigns that belittle their chosen means of getting around (Figure 1.2). It is that same marginal social status that animates the broader bike movement's political agenda to fight for bicycle accommodations on city streets, and to take on a corporate giant like General Motors when it communicates an anti-bicycle message.

Fieldwork on Two Wheels: Pedaling Toward Critical Estrangement

Since I first learned how to ride one around age five, bicycles have played a large role in my life. I've spent countless hours pedaling a bicycle on and off roads (for exercise, in competitions, running errands, in parades and protests, touring country roads, raising money for charities), working on them (as a mechanic of my own and other peoples' bikes), and advocating for them in local and national transportation politics. I think of myself a "cyclist," that is, as someone who prioritizes the bicycle in my lifestyle (relatively few who ride bicycles think of themselves as "cyclists," by the way; Grant 2012), and my social circles include others who consider themselves "cyclists." But I had not really given any thought to approaching bicycles anthropologically until a few years ago when two things became apparent to me. One of these is that in my research on cultures of environmentalism that I've been involved in for almost two decades, I found increasing attention given to the greening of transportation, and a tendency to celebrate the bicycle as an environmentally-virtuous vehicle. The other is the noticeable growth of bicycle riders on the streets of the city in which I live and work, Burlington, Vermont, and in nearby cities such as

Figure 1.2 **One Way to Promote Bicycle Safety.**
Credit: Hulton Collection

Montreal, Boston, and New York. Curious about what might be behind these changes and whether they might be connected—In what ways is riding a bicycle green? Are people riding them as a statement of environmental values or politics, or is it something else? What is happening in cities right now that they might want to promote bicycles and other alternative means of transportation?—I began a series of casual conversations with others who ride bicycles, as well as bicycle advocates, urban planners, environmental activists, and others that has grown into a full-blown research project on the intersections of bicycles and urban mobility based on ethnographic fieldwork in my own city and other locations where bicycle mobility is on local agendas of urban change. Important parts of this book, especially part of Chapter 3 and all of Chapter 4, are drawn from this fieldwork, and even in sections that draw from the published works of others, this ethnographic background informs my understanding of what they are saying.

The opportunity to conduct ethnographic fieldwork in my own city of Burlington seemed especially ripe to me, because it has been undergoing the kind of bicycle renaissance happening elsewhere and when people talk about what's happening here, they situate it as part of broader regional, national— even global—shifts in how many people relate to everyday mobility. The fact that Vermont ranks second in the country for overall rates of bicycling and walking (Alliance for Biking & Walking 2012) confirmed my sense that there was a good opportunity to do research among cyclists. In my fieldwork I have sought out those social spaces in Burlington in which people spend time talking about and riding bicycles, listening to what they have to say about their lives with bicycles, paying close attention to what they do with those bicycles, and trying to understand how riding a bicycle, making, selling or buying a bicycle, and advocating for bicycle use are socially organized activities. The settings for this fieldwork have been bicycle shops, machine shops where bicycles are manufactured, bicycle advocacy organization offices and workshops, a community bicycle shop with an earn-a-bike program, public meetings and presentations where bicycle and other mobility issues are debated and discussed, bicycle festivals and shows, transportation conferences, and on streets themselves where people are actually riding bicycles. Bicycles, like cars, are a form of private mobility which means that people often ride alone and do not typically congregate consciously and deliberately *as bicycle riders*. Nevertheless, the streets themselves become contexts in which people and their bicycles interact, and so I have also become a keen observer of city streets, bike lanes, intersections, and sidewalks. I have also been active in local bicycle politics, as an advocate promoting better conditions for bicycle users, and related to that work, I have attended regional and national bike advocacy conferences not just as an advocate but as an ethnographer. In all of these settings, I've interacted with and interviewed bike shop owners, mechanics, salespeople, customers, bicycle activists, bike commuters, city planners and other public officials concerned with transportation, and, most of all, men and women riders of different ages, social classes, and ethnicities.

Maybe it goes without saying, but I have done much of this local fieldwork using a bicycle. Some of the time, this use is nothing more than getting myself to and from the settings in which I am conducting fieldwork or doing an interview. But having a bicycle also means taking a bicycle into a shop for parts or repairs, interacting with others (albeit often briefly) on the roads, even simply riding a bicycle through city streets, each of which can become a setting for research as my own intimate and embodied experience becomes the basis for generating insights into bicycle mobility and making sense of what others are saying about it. Among the many dozens of people I've interviewed, observed, and interacted with in this research are friends, neighbors, and acquaintances who, like me, are passionate (or maybe just curious) about bicycles. My identity as an ethnographer doing research is difficult to separate from who I am as a "native" involved in various ways with bicycles in my own city. This fieldwork process has also been quite episodic and fluid, as I've tried to balance this research with my professional obligations as a university professor and as a father with three young children.

Anthropology has historically had a keen interest in far-flung places, and has well-developed concepts and tools for understanding cross-cultural differences. But the decision to conduct ethnographic fieldwork "at home" is not at all unique these days. As anthropologist Micaela di Leonardo (1998: 367) once wrote, "American anthropologists need not go home again; we have always been there." Although di Leonardo's deeper point is that anthropology's historic quest to study "exotic Others" around the world has helped shape American notions about cultural difference, it is possible to take her point more literally: anthropologists have been conducting fieldwork "at home" since at least the 1930s when Hortense Powdermaker, a pioneering American anthropologist and student of Bronislaw Malinowski, decided to study race relations in Alabama (Vivanco 2010).

Still, the notion of traveling to conduct research far away and staying there continuously for a long period of time remains central to disciplinary ideas about fieldwork. It is hard to say when one "becomes an anthropologist," but pursuing fieldwork away is a major rite of passage. Showing that one has conducted fieldwork abroad is a matter of prestige—in some circles, the further afield one goes, the greater the prestige (Gupta and Ferguson 1997)—and has important consequences for one's employability in an anthropology department, where faculty positions are often tied to expertise in a particular world region.

But this vision of ethnographic fieldwork is based on the questionable idea that doing anthropology requires one to "set off for the field," that is, make a physical and social break with home to become immersed, with a singularity of focus and purpose, in the face-to-face relationships of a particular group of people (Amit 2000). It imagines "the field" as an independently bounded set of relationships and activities to be discovered. Yet in a world of incessant motion and overlapping social and political-economic connections, in which people, goods, ideas, money, media, and other forces seem to flow in all directions across the planet, it is practically impossible to imagine any community as isolated, bounded, and waiting "to be discovered." The internet adds a new dimension of interconnectedness to many peoples' lives, also creating new opportunities for anthropological research. These opportunities have extended to this project, where in addition to the kinds of research settings discussed above, I have been observing and interacting in online fora, blogs, YouTube, websites, Twitter feeds, and other media environments where everyday bicycle mobility is being discussed, demonstrated, and debated.

It is also good to be skeptical of the image of fieldworker as singularly dedicated and immersed. My own experience conducting over 20 months of fieldwork on environmentalism and ecotourism in rural Costa Rica during the 1990s (Vivanco 2006) speaks directly to this point. Although that experience otherwise fits into disciplinary ideals of long-term fieldwork in a distant community, I was hardly "continuously immersed": family and friends often came to visit, I was in regular contact with advisors and colleagues back home through phone and email, I spent a lot of time creating a relationship with my future wife who was also living there, and I came and went from the community in which I lived for all kinds of reasons, including heading to the capital to do interviews, archival research, and get access to media materials helpful for my research. Long after my time there ended, my fieldwork continued through phone conversations, email, internet chatrooms, websites, and visits here in the U.S. with people I had met there.

So the "field" is not necessarily a given place to which anthropologists travel; it is a constructed set of relationships and social settings that every anthropologist who conducts ethnographic research works hard to identify, create, and cultivate (Amit 2000: 6). Ethnographic fieldwork is thus a lot messier and more open-ended than it appears in the books and articles we write. It is, as I said above about the fieldwork involved in writing this book, episodic and fluid. The division between the ethnographer and the native can get blurry. We meld our personal and professional roles and identities. Although we call them "informants"—something that sounds quite formal and distancing—the reality is that a lot of the people we draw our richest information, knowledge, perspectives, and analyses from are friends, neighbors, associates, and contacts with whom we might have intermittent, serendipitous, diffuse, even sometimes ephemeral ties. What defines ethnographic fieldwork is thus not in the act of separation from our everyday lives to immerse ourselves continuously in intensive social life elsewhere, but the deliberate work of creating contacts and interactions that yield meaningful insights into human lives without assuming that the ethnographer stands apart from these processes.

Another key distinction about ethnographic fieldwork here involves what John Comaroff (2010: 530) has called "critical estrangement of the lived world," or the work of taking the familiar and taken-for-granted and making it seem strange, of "deconstructing its surfaces and the relativizing of its horizons." Going beneath the contours of everyday existence opens up new opportunities to think critically about the historical and social dynamics that shape peoples' lives and ways of thinking. Perhaps achieving this distancing sounds like it implies some kind of mental trick. How does one distance oneself from intimate experience and taken-for-granted categories? How can I take a step back from my own lifestyle as a cyclist to think critically about the bicycle and its role in everyday mobility, or as one of my colleagues once asked me, "how can you study the parade if you're marching in it?"

Comaroff, who notes that this issue goes "way back" to the beginnings of anthropology, observes that critical estrangement is based not on mental trickery but in two maneuvers that define the uniqueness of the anthropological perspective. One of these is a comparative approach based on considering particular details of human behavior or thought against the backdrop of historical or cross-cultural awareness of how people in other places and times might behave or think. The feeling of naturalness of our way of doing things immediately dissipates when you realize another group of people take or took for granted something completely different. The comparative approach almost inevitably forces one to confront one's own taken-for-granted assumptions, as well, a process that can be kick-started right now, in Box 1.2. The other lies in keeping a key question at the forefront of our minds, which Comaroff (2010: 530) expresses this way: "What is it that actually gives substance to the dominant discourses and conventional practices of that world, to its subject positions and its semiosis, its received categories and their unruly undersides, to the manner in which it is perceived and experienced, fabricated, and contested?" In other words, what social, cultural, and historical conditions give rise to and help sustain a particular set of ideas, meanings, objects, or social practices?

Box 1.2 Beginning to Step Back from the Bicycle

The bicycle holds implicit and unspoken meanings for all of us that are the product of our own individual experiences with bicycles, as well as shared cultural perspectives toward them. Americans' tacit meanings of the bicycle tend to categorize them around themes of childhood, recreation, and competition. I've found in the course of my research that people like to tell stories about bicycles, many even get animated about it even if they haven't ridden a bicycle in years, and that most of these stories involve our shared cultural associations of bicycles with those themes. So I've heard lots of stories about vivid childhood memories in which a bicycle played a role, about how a childhood gift of a bicycle was a rite of passage into responsibility or freedom, about family bonding around fun bicycle rides, and about the bicycle's role in developing personal control, resilience, or endurance. At the same time that these stories align closely with those dominant cultural associations of bicycling with kids and sports, they can also (but not necessarily) suppress or downplay other ways of thinking of bicycles, such as the idea of the bicycle as a practical vehicle for everyday life. It's not that individuals cannot rethink their tacit meanings; people do it often, and cultures are quite flexible and dynamic.

The problem for the anthropologist studying one's own culture is that these kinds of tacit meanings and assumptions can get in the way of understanding others' tacit meanings when we are not sufficiently self-reflexive about how culture and its meanings shape our own perceptions. Dislodging those (what anthropologist Edward Sapir in 1921 called) "well-worn grooves of expression" can be difficult—some would say impossible—but beginning to do an anthropological analysis of anything begins with taking a step back to try to recognize how our own thinking as individuals reflects, and is shaped by, certain shared patterns and tacit meanings of our own culture (Sapir 1921).

Opportunities for Reflection and Action

As a first step back from the bicycle, a free-writing exercise can be useful to expose some the tacit meanings that inform how you see the bicycle. It is especially useful if several others are doing this exercise as well, as you can compare stories. You should each write at least one page on a significant event or situation involving a bicycle that seems particularly meaningful to you. Swap papers several times so that you have a chance to read others' stories. Do any patterns, themes, or topics emerge in these stories and why do you think they emerge? How does your story relate to broader cultural associations of the bicycle with childhood, recreation, or competition? If it doesn't, why not?

This book might be thought of as a practical exercise in anthropological critical estrangement. Through a holistic anthropological lens, it shows how historical events, cultural perspectives, social processes, and political-economic dynamics have shaped not just how people have thought about, interacted with, produced, bought, and sold bicycles, but also how cityscapes and shifting attitudes toward the appropriate technologies for moving around them are currently being rethought because of concerns raised in contexts of rapid social and environmental change. It will reveal the ways structures of power operate in daily life, as well as efforts to develop viable social and environmentally sustainable alternatives. Chapter 2 begins with a simple yet beguiling question, "what (and when) is a bicycle?," the goal being to demonstrate some of the techniques involved in developing that critical estrangement when dealing with ordinary objects. This chapter will also carry us through a brief history of bicycle technology. Chapter 3 examines the cultures of bicycle use in three distinct urban contexts, Burlington, Amsterdam, and Bogotá, to situate both the particular dynamics shaping how and why bicycles have emerged in those places as important vehicles of everyday life, but also the globally interconnected discussions and dialogues over urban change that inform how and why bicycles have emerged in those places. This chapter asks who is riding and why, and how bicycles are used in different ways in processes of cultural expression. In Chapter 4, I explore ethnographically the emergence of a social movement around bicycling, focusing on the specific challenges and strategies bicycle advocates are currently using not just to make space for bicycles on urban streets, but the struggles they confront in trying to change accepted meanings and practices of what a bicycle is in their work. In the conclusion, I consider various perspectives on the need for the bicycle in the context of a summary of this book's major points.

For Further Exploration

To actually view the GM ad and some responses in the bicycle blogging community, see here: http://bikeportland.org/2011/10/11/gm-ad-urges-college-students-to-stop-pedaling-start-driving-60399. Giant's response to GM's original ad is here: http://bikeportland.org/2011/10/13/giant-remakes-gm-ad-and-other-reactions-to-the-fiasco-60505

In the fairly large social science literature on the impacts of automobility on American culture, landscapes, politics, and economics, one book stands out: *Carjacked* by Catherine Lutz and Ann Lutz Fernandez. It is both highly readable and, uniquely, it approaches Americans' relationships with cars through the lens of culture (Catherine is a cultural anthropologist). They note that, like many elements of culture, the car "is what we see *with* rather than *what* we see" (2010: 11). The book has a useful and thought-provoking website here: http://www.carjacked.org/. This book pairs usefully with a reading of John Urry's influential book on the rise of a mobility paradigm in the social sciences, *Mobilities* (http://www.polity.co.uk/book.asp?ref=9780745634180).

For an excellent overview of why bicycles have been on the rise in urban areas throughout the Americas and Europe, the film *Contested Streets: Breaking New York City Gridlock* offers comparative perspectives of the role of bicycles in rethinking the politics and daily experiences of urban mobility. A trailer of the film and information about its purchase are available at http://www.contestedstreets.org/.

Research on bicycles in the social sciences is still sparse, but in the past several years it has been gaining steam as this article attests: http://www.psmag.com/education/bicycle-studies-pick-up-speed-in-academia-43660/. One of the central texts is the volume *Cycling and Society*, edited by well-known bicycle social scientists

Dave Horton, Peter Cox, and Paul Rosen (http://www.ashgate.com/default. aspx?page=637&calcTitle=1&title_id=8469&edition_id=9721&lang=cy-GB).

There are also several conferences where bike researchers gather and share their findings, including The International Cycling History conference (http://www. cycling-history.org/) whose proceedings are published in the journal *Bicycle History* (http://www.cycling-history.org/), and the World Cycling Research Forum (http://www.wocref.org/index.html) whose proceedings are published in the journal *Cycling Research International* (http://www.wocref.org/CRI.html). Every year, the Velo City conference takes place somewhere around the world, and although it is primarily oriented toward urban planning some social scientists present their research there (http://www.velo-city2012.com/).

Although not really discussed in this chapter, the conduct of ethnographic research involves significant moral and ethical questions, and as a profession anthropologists follow the American Anthropological Association's Code of Ethics, found here: http://www.aaanet.org/committees/ethics/ethcode.htm.

2

WHAT (AND WHEN) IS A BICYCLE?

What is a bicycle? If you imagined something like this:

> A bicycle is a vehicle composed of two wheels one behind another held by a diamond-shaped frame, propelled by pedals and steered with handlebars attached to the front wheel,

you wouldn't necessarily be incorrect. This description is (more or less) the one you are likely to find in a contemporary dictionary, and in fact, it describes in common sensical terms what most of us accept to be a bicycle.

But anthropologists tend to be cautious around common sense, mainly because common sense has often proven to be neither common nor sensical. That is, what you and I take for granted to be "a bicycle" may not be universally accepted as the only way to define it, or blurrier than we think because our own images of it differ from the more complex realities of the object itself. Consider, for example, the two things pictured in Figures 2.1 and 2.2, an electric bicycle and a recumbent bicycle.

Electric bicycles are one of the fastest growing segments of global bicycle markets, appealing precisely because they use a motor to accentuate or replace altogether the act of propulsion by pedaling. Their status as hybrid vehicles, somewhere between self-powered and motorized, as well as the rapid speeds they can travel, is currently raising difficult questions for governments about how to classify and regulate them for use on city streets because they don't necessarily act like bicycles are supposed to act. As for the recumbent bicycle, it seems to fit the definition above in the broadest terms, though its unique handlebar position, its differently sized wheels, the elongated shape of the frame, the orientation of the seat, and the placement of the cranks and pedals defy easy categorization. Perhaps, in the end, we can accept that these are "bicycles" because they meet the general spirit of our definition above, but what should we make of the object in Figure 2.3? It is a three-wheeled recumbent cycle called a "velomobile" whose adherents argue passionately (and with good reason) that its speed, efficiency, ability to overcome air resistance, stability, and

Figure 2.1 **Electric Bicycle.**
Credit: Fotosearch

Figure 2.2 **Recumbent Bicycle.**
Credit: © 2001 Getty Images

Figure 2.3 **Velomobile.**
Credit: © Bonnier Corp

comfort make it superior to the object defined above for riding long distances or in fast-moving automobile traffic (Wilson 2004).

Even as the word "bicycle" signifies something, that *thing* it refers to is not as static and unidimensional as any definition implies. These complexities can become apparent when we bring the thing itself into the foreground, instead of consigning it to the background, which is what we tend to do with things we take for granted. The bicycle has taken and continues to take diverse forms, forms that are intertwined with complex histories of technological innovation, industrial capitalism, political-economic dynamics, consumerism, and social change. The reason the thing defined at the outset of this chapter has become most common is not due solely to its technological characteristics but also to the ways it became accepted within important social and institutional processes. The first part of this chapter explores these dynamics through a brief history of the bicycle, suggesting that one possible answer to the question posed by this chapter—what is a bicycle?—is closely related to the *when* of a bicycle, that is, its historical period and the diverse social and technical factors that influenced the shape and qualities of the object.

Building on this history, the second part of the chapter explores the multidimensional character of bicycles as objects, with the goal of addressing our central question from a more conceptual and contemporary angle. This section proposes that understanding what a bicycle is requires attention to the complex interplay of physical possibilities and constraints set by the object itself, its relationship with other objects, the meanings and intentions people bring to it, the ways it affects and changes peoples' experiences and perceptions, and the cultural meanings and social organization surrounding its practical use. Here, addressing the *when* of a bicycle is also relevant in considering the *what* of a bicycle, requiring the identification of an individual bicycle's past, present, and future connected to its production, exchange, and temporal conditions of use. The conceptual approach laid out here could be applied to many other everyday objects, so one goal will be to highlight the particularities involved in people–bicycle relationships.

Together, the two distinct parts of this chapter demonstrate that the bicycle is a complex socio-technical object whose meanings and uses are shaped variously through its histories, production, and uses. What does this matter for understanding the role of bicycles in everyday mobility? For one, it can help us explore how "matter matters," that is, to begin to specify the role material things play in shaping expectations, concepts, practices, and experiences involved in the ordinary practice of getting around. Second, understanding these historical and conceptual details can help cultivate the kind of critical estrangement discussed in the first chapter. "Making the bicycle strange" reveals that the ways people have perceived, experienced, fabricated, and argued over the bicycle and its role in everday mobility are closely tied to particular contexts of time and place. Third, and perhaps most important, it can help generate a critical perspective on a deep-seated cultural framework that informs most Americans' views of bicycles, as technologically static and obsolete vehicles inferior to more "advanced" vehicles such as motorcycles and cars, and thus not suitable for serious transportation but "less serious" pursuits like recreation, exercise, or child's play (Cox and Van De Walle 2007).

Part One: A Brief History of Bicycles

Bicycles originated in and between northern Europe and the United States during the nineteenth century. Conventional histories of the bicycle—"bicycle" being a word that came into use during the 1860s—tend to focus on the bicycle as a design object, tracking changes in its form and components over time, or explaining changes in its manufacture from small-scale craft workshops in its early decades to full-scale industrial production by the 1890s (Herlihy 2004; Epperson 2010). Bicycles were among the very first—and most expensive— mass-produced luxury durable consumer goods in the U.S. and Europe, and so these histories can tell us a lot about how, where, and why industrial firms practicing mass production emerged, as well as the creation of new consumer markets to generate desire for these products. Bicycles were also tied closely with important Victorian-era social transformations, including women's rights, the emergence of a "good roads" movement promoting better quality roads and streets, and the rise of the automobile. The stress in these histories is on the technical development of the bicycle and its impacts on society. Although bicycle historians continue to debate the details, in its most general form the conventional history of the bicycle recognizes three distinct phases and general cycle types: the velocipede, the high-wheeler, and the safety bicycle.

The Velocipede

In 1815, a volcano on the island of Sumbawa in what is now Indonesia spewed huge amounts of ash into the upper atmosphere, blocking solar radiation into the next year, resulting in the famous "year without summer" of 1816. Global temperatures dropped during those twelve months, and in places as far afield as New England and northern Europe crisis broke out as snow fell in July, harvests failed, and farmers faced economic ruin. With oat prices soaring, some farmers in southern Germany apparently began to kill their horses because they couldn't feed them (Penn 2011). In this context a concerned German nobleman named Baron Karl von Drais de Sauerbronn, a tinkerer who had already been working on his dream of inventing a horseless carriage, conceived the idea of a mechanical horse with wheels (Herlihy 2004; Penn 2011). Unveiled in 1817, von Drais called his horse-replacement vehicle a "Laufmaschine" (running machine), which later became known variously as the "velocipede," "Draisine," and "hobby horse" (Figure 2.4). It was basic from our modern vantage point, having rudimentary steering, no pedals (the user propelled it by running with the legs while straddled over the thing), and was rather dangerous and uncomfortable since there were no brakes; at the time, carriage roads could be quite bumpy and rutted. Going down hills, the rider simply lifted his legs and hoped for the best. Even still, its speed was impressive compared to walking (eight to ten miles per hour), and a number of wealthy and fashionable men in England, the U.S., France, and Germany took a liking to them and learned the techniques of using them in newly opened indoor riding schools.

Initial interest in the Draisine velocipede was brief, although for several decades it continued to enjoy short bursts of popularity in northern Europe and the U.S. In the early 1860s, a young machinist working in a Paris cart and buggy shop named Pierre Lallemont conceived of adding cranks with pedals to the front wheel of a Draisine that had been brought in for repair, wanting to know if it was possible to balance, steer, and pedal the device simultaneously (Bjiker 1995; Epperson 2010). He soon moved to Connecticut, where he built a new velocipede and was reportedly arrested for riding it around New Haven (Epperson 2010). He secured a U.S. patent for his invention but could not interest any manufacturers in it, so in 1868 he returned to Paris. On his return

Figure 2.4 **Draisine. Racing Olympics on Draisines.**
Credit: The Bridgeman Art Library

he learned that the device he had begun developing years earlier had caught on in his absence, and several French firms were producing versions of the pedal-driven velocipede, including the Michaux brothers (his former employers) whose firm had become the first prominent bicycle manufacturer in existence. Interest in the velocipede spread to the U.S. in 1868 when a well-known troupe of gymnasts used one in their traveling act, and the fad of velocipede riding (now also called "bicycle" riding) took off along the East Coast, especially New York City (Bjiker 1995; Epperson 2010). Ice skating rinks were converted to riding schools, though when riders took the device outside they discovered that the sheer weight of the vehicle (as much as 150 pounds) and its iron carriage wheels made it difficult and uncomfortable on irregular roads and city sidewalks (where they were quickly banned), earning for the velocipede the nickname "boneshaker" (Figure 2.5).

The High-Wheeler

Although some American carriage makers began making them, interest in boneshakers quickly died out. A new generation of bicycles was being created in small blacksmith and carriage shops, mostly in England and France, to increase speed. The new designs were based on using lighter weight frame materials and, since these were direct-drive vehicles, making the front wheel larger to make them go faster. However, as these front wheels grew in diameter, their weight

Figure 2.5 **Boneshaker Velocipede, circa 1869.**
Credit: Getty Images

became a problem and attention soon fell on developing new lightweight and more forgiving wheels based on using thin wire spokes with uniform spoke tension, the same concept we see in bicycle wheels today. By 1871, these new bicycles sported very large front wheels with solid rubber tires and smaller rear wheels, becoming known as "Ordinary" or "High-wheel" bicycles (Figure 2.6). The Franco-Prussian War (1870–1871) interrupted Continental interest in cycling, and the center of bicycle production shifted to sewing machine factories in England where steel frames and parts could be built.

The high-wheelers were the first real successful bicycles in the U.S. and the U.K., although their expense (a month's typical wages or more) limited them to the wealthy. During the 1880s a craze nevertheless erupted that was fueled by greater availability of high wheelers, and the rise of bicycle racing as a popular spectator sport. Fashionable and proper gentlemen—for they were *men*, since women rarely rode high-wheelers—joined "wheelmen's clubs," elite social clubs of prominent citizens modeled on cavalry units in which members "wheeled" through cities and toured the countryside, dressed in military-style uniforms and organized in ranks and formations (Herlihy 2004; Mackintosh and Norcliffe 2007). Wheeling was viewed as a social activity with important rules, and those who didn't join clubs but rode as individuals were derided as "scorchers," a threatening figure whose practice of speeding through towns, cities, and rural

Figure 2.6 **Ordinary, circa 1889.**
Source: Courtesy of Glenn Eames

roads broke rules of urban propriety and generated a lot of antagonism among horsemen and pedestrians.

One of the key figures in expanding cycling during this time was a U.S. Civil War veteran from Boston named Col. Albert Pope, who was first exposed to British high wheelers in 1876 at the Philadelphia Centennial Exposition. He decided to import some for sale, and in 1877, seeing a major business opportunity, arranged for a Connecticut sewing machine company to begin mass producing high wheelers under his new brand name, Columbia. As Pope's success grew, his company Columbia Bicycles would take over the sewing machine firm, expand the factory, and become the largest bicycle manufacturer in the world. Although a handful of other American firms also began manufacturing high wheelers, throughout the 1880s Pope helped grow the market for cycling in the U.S. through clever advertising and by founding and bankrolling a national organization in 1880—the League of American Wheelmen (L.A.W.)—to fight for the legal right to use bicycles in public spaces (most famously New York's Central Park, where they were initially banned). Even more important, recognizing that bicycling required smooth road surfaces, the L.A.W. launched a national "good roads" movement to lobby national and state governments to take over responsibility for road maintenance from cities and towns, which were inconsistent in their commitments to maintaining roads.

The Safety Bicycle

Although notable feats of speed and endurance were accomplished with high-wheelers—including the first bicycle ride around the world by Englishman Thomas Stevens in the late 1880s—they were dangerous and awkward bicycles. They were hard to mount, difficult to stop even with brakes, and when they hit ubiquitous potholes could end up in what became known as "headers," as the rider pitched over the front wheel, sometimes to his death. Recognizing these downsides, in 1885, Englishman James Starley—who had played a major role in developing the high-wheelers—developed a new bicycle he called the "safety bicycle" (Figure 2.7). This bicycle was safer and easier to ride, with two equally sized wheels (which soon sported pneumatic tires, invented by Irish doctor John Dunlop in 1888), a saddle resting on a diamond-shaped steel frame between them, and propelled by pedals connected to a sprocket and chain that attached to the rear wheel. This design is the same basic design we see today in most bicycles.

Figure 2.7 **Rover Safety Bicycle, 1885.**
Credit: © SSPL/Science Museum

As the 1890s began, Pope and an increasing number of other manufacturers in the U.S., Britain, France, and Germany recognized significant opportunities to promote safety bicycles among men, as well as a new segment of the market, women. By the end of the 1890s—which has become known as the period of "first bicycle boom"—bicycle manufacturing had become an important and prestigious industry, especially in the U.S., and somewhere between 2 and 4 million Americans, 1 million people in Britain and France each, and a half million in Germany were riding safety bicycles (Petty 1995). In the U.S. alone, over 300 manufacturing firms produced a total of 1.1 million bicycles by 1899 (Aronson 1952).

Critical to the success of the safety bicycle were innovations in how bicycles were made, innovations designed primarily to increase the efficiency of manufacture and reduce the cost to the consumer—although throughout the decade bicycles remained expensive luxury goods still available mostly to upper and middle classes. The U.S. bicycle industry—now well beyond its roots in the blacksmith and carriage shops—was at the cutting edge of these changes, combining a New England tradition of armories and small machine manufacture with Western manufacturing of big farm machines (Epperson 2010). In the process it pioneered new forms of vertically-integrated mass production based on economies of scale, practices that would quickly spread to other industries (Norcliffe 1997). Pope's company Columbia, in particular, divided work in an assembly-line fashion, in which specialized departments performed specific jobs and sent their pieces to another unit to be assembled with other parts. It also made key advances in metallurgy, welding techniques, ball-bearing production, the use of standard and interchangeable parts, and ways of making steel tubing. Pope's maxim—"the perfection of the machine lessened the number of employees" (quoted in Norcliffe 1997: 274)—led to the development of important new machines for stamping and pressing steel and other tasks. Thomas Edison was even hired to electrify Pope's factory to create a continuously moving assembly line and to provide lighting for night shifts, both of which were firsts for mass production. Henry Ford, who began his career as a bicycle mechanic, reportedly visited Pope's factory and gained a lot of ideas about mass production that he would later implement in his own automobile factory (Norcliffe 1997). The unprecedented growth and successes of bicycle manufacturing promoted a corresponding growth in industrial workers' unions, bicycle repair shops, riding instruction schools, and firms producing bicycle accessories such as lights, saddles, bells, and clothing (Aronson 1952).

The growing popularity of bicycles during the 1890s was not due solely to industrial advances. Bicycling gained new meanings as a status symbol for the upper and middle classes, endowing its practitioners with social distinction as progressive and modern. It was also viewed as a liberating activity that promoted "auto-mobility," a form of pleasurable self-empowerment, independent movement, mastery over self and machine, and effortless speed (Ebert 2004; Furness 2010).[1] At the same time, bicycles offered new possibilities for leisurely outings to the countryside and neighboring towns, representing a means of recreation and escape from dirty and crowded cities. Horses, many people began to believe, had become obsolete: unlike horses, bicycles did not have a mind of their own, did not get tired or require expensive feed and housing, or leave large quantities of droppings and urine on city streets (Herlihy 2004; Macy 2010).

But the bicycle's rising popularity was not met without social controversy and opposition. Pedestrians and horsemen continued to see bicyclists as a nuisance. One of the great medical debates of the decade was over bicycling's health consequences. While some doctors declared bicycling to be almost miraculous in its health-giving properties, others warned darkly of bicycle-related maladies like tuberculosis, uncontrollable desires to have sex, and "bicycle face," a contortion of the face born of the struggle to balance a bicycle (Pridmore and Hurd 1995; Herlihy 2004). Some religious leaders joined in with their own concerns, condemning bicycle riding as promoting moral decay, especially on Sundays which would be better spent in church.

Controversy also surrounded growing enthusiasm for bicycling among women. At a time when young upper- and middle-class women were strictly supervised in public, bicycle riding allowed the "new woman" of the 1890s an unprecedented degree of unchaperoned freedom and independence. Although bicycle manufacturers began producing step-through frames that were easier for women in dresses to mount and ride, bicycling fueled dissatisfaction over restrictive corsets and dresses of the era. This dissatisfaction led to the use of "bloomers" (athletic pants that allowed for discrete mounting and dismounting of a bicycle) and a "rational clothing" movement that advocated for shorter dresses and other changes to allow for freer movement (Macy 2011). These new ideas represented a major challenge to the social norms of the time, and provoked moral outrage, even among women. As the female head of the Women's Rescue League in the U.S., a prominent group working for the rights of female workers, warned, "Bicycling by young women has helped to swell the ranks of restless girls who finally drift into the standing army of outcast women" (Macy 2011: 28). At the same time, the bicycle had gained important champions in the women's suffrage movement that was fighting for more freedoms and the right to vote for women, including the author and activist Elizabeth Cady Stanton, who once wrote "The bicycle will inspire women with more courage, self-respect, and self-reliance and will make the next generation more vigorous of mind and of body; for feeble mothers do not produce great statesmen, scientists and scholars" (quoted in Macy 2011: 77–78). Even the famed American suffragette leader Susan B. Anthony weighed in, declaring in 1896,

"Let me tell what I think of bicycling. I think it has done more to emancipate women than anything else in the world. I stand and I rejoice every time I see a woman ride by on a wheel" (quoted in Macy 2011: 77).

Much has been made of the fact that the mass production and use of safety bicycles contributed directly to the rise of the automobile during this same period (Aronson 1952; Herlihy 2004; Furness 2010). As bicycle historian Aronson (1952: 310) observed, "The bicycle did the dirty work for its mechanized successor in a variety of ways." These include innovative manufacturing processes and machines developed for bicycle factories, such as the adoption of assembly-line production methods using standardized parts. (Indeed, after experiencing much success in mass producing bicycles, Pope himself began mass producing automobiles, thought it was canceled by his death; Norcliffe 1997) Specific technological innovations developed for bicycles—among them pneumatic tires, ball bearings, and steel tubing—were also picked up for use in automobiles. Another key element was the fact that bicycling helped create infrastructure necessary to support the automobile, especially a network of repair shops with trained mechanics (many early automobile repair shops began as bicycle repair businesses), and a good roads movement convincing Americans to change the way road projects and maintenance were funded and built. There was a legal dimension here as well: new legal mechanisms had been developed to regulate bicycles, from headlight laws to speed limits, and police departments developed systems of enforcement to control and punish riders for traffic infractions. Perhaps most important, the bicycle laid the foundation for a new concept of personal mobility that is taken for granted today not just among automobile drivers but, quite simply as "modern" condition, a notion that emphasizes the freedom of individual movement and speed with minimal effort (Rosen 2002; Furness 2010).

By the first years of the twentieth century, the first bicycle boom had petered out as supply outstripped demand in European and American markets. But the safety bicycle had proven both its appeal and utility beyond the upper and middle classes, and in the coming decades, safety bicycle technology spread among social masses throughout the world. During the early and mid-twentieth century, even as automobiles began to overtake bicycles as modern and freedom-giving vehicles, safety bicycles became commonplace vehicles for the transportation of people and goods throughout numerous European countries and, through the exportation of European-made bicycles, to their colonies and former colonies in Africa, Latin America, and Asia (Nwabughuogu 1984; Pivato 1990; Carstensen and Ebert 2012). Some countries, especially India in the mid-1940s and China after the Communist Revolution in 1949, constructed their own domestic industries based on safety bicycle technology to promote economic development and inexpensive popular transportation (Moghaddaas

2003; Panday 2009). In many countries, the use of safety bicycles on a mass scale for everyday transportation remains commonplace.

In the U.S., the story is radically different given how the systematic reorganization of transportation patterns around mass public transit and, beginning in the 1920s, mass automobilization, marginalized the bicycle as a transportation choice (Herlihy 2004; Jones 2008). Except for the persistence of urban bicycle messengers in major cities, bicycle use dropped substantially among adults and shifted toward children, offering those not yet able to drive a cheap, convenient, and independent means to get to school, run errands, and explore (Herlihy 2004: 325). Throughout the middle decades of the twentieth-century, bicycles produced in the U.S. became heavier and adopted decorative elements associated with automobiles, such as gas tanks. Post-WWII suburbanization organized around automobile transportation and highway construction further marginalized the bicycle, although by the 1960s, the bicycle began to enjoy a new period of popularity and ushered in a "second bicycle boom" that peaked with millions of bicycles sold in the early 1970s. The rise of the bicycle in this period was fueled by a shift toward the production of lighter-weight European-style "ten speed" bicycles that catered to emerging adult interest in exercise and health-conscious recreation as well as—especially after the 1973 OPEC oil embargo—concern over high gasoline prices. Many people returned to their cars, however, after gas prices began falling in the late 1970s, and with weakening consumer demand, a number of major U.S. bicycle manufacturers entered into terminal decline. Only the unexpected rise of the mountain bike in the 1980s revived the bicycle industry's fortunes during the 1990s and its qualities as a practical, rugged, and comfortable bicycle for urban use laid the foundations for the current bicycle boom in some urban areas (Rosen 2002). Throughout this history, not just in the U.S. but across the world, one thing has remained pretty much constant: all of these bicycles were versions of the safety bicycle introduced in the 1880s and popularized in the 1890s.

Is the Safety Bicycle the Pinnacle of Bicycle "Evolution"?

You may have noticed that until now, I have not used the term "evolution" to describe the bicycle's origins and development. Yet the way conventional histories of the bicycle are told is typically based on a narrative in which a succession of technological modifications and refinements reached their apex by the 1890s with the safety bicycle, and, the argument goes, bicycles and their design haven't really changed much since then. Following an evolutionary line of thinking, the reason we still see that basic design today is due to its advantages over previous cycle designs. Further, the assumption goes, there was no good reason to continue improving the bicycle once it reached its "finished" state. The logical conclusions are that the development of pedal-powered machines long ago reached a pinnacle, stagnated, and, eclipsed by more technologically-advanced motorized vehicles like motorcycles and automobiles, became an anachronistic and outmoded transportation technology (Cox and Van De Walle 2007). Pulling back from the bicycle itself, this basic narrative of techno-logical change is a familiar one, a central ideology of contemporary consumer culture being that technology "evolves." The result is technological hierarchy, in which the fittest designs and artifacts survive, win out, or are privileged because of their inherent competitive superiority.

But processes of technological innovation and change, as well as the persistence of certain technologies and objects, are not so simple. Technological development rarely (if ever) follows a linear "evolutionary" path, because innovation and change are subject to a diverse array of contingencies and influences (Bjiker 1995; Pels et al. 2002). One set of influences is the technical worlds of objects, their components, and the processes necessary or available to manufacture them, which have an important bearing on what is possible to create, manufacture, and bring to market. Importantly, however, these pro-cesses do not take place in social, cultural, political, or economic isola-tion (Bjiker 1995). The social and cultural worlds and decisions of actors associated with particular technologies—inventors, designers, engineers, manufacturers, investors, promoters, advertisers, policy-makers, various user groups, etc.— are just as important in shaping technological outcomes (Bjiker 1995; Rosen 2002).

For example, for 50 years, von Drais' velocipede was a largely irrelevant curi-osity. Although there were periodic outbursts of enthusiasm surrounding it, there were neither appropriate physical infrastructure in roads nor sustained social acceptance of this vehicle to make that enthusiasm grow or last beyond a very small community. Beginning in the 1860s, the bicycle's development was enabled by the economic infrastructure and labor conditions of the carriage-making and blacksmithing shops; reliant on socioeconomic elites willing and able to invest not just in the expensive machine but also in the time and effort necessary to develop the skills for riding one; and bedeviled by poor roads and legal prohibitions on riding. The problem of substandard roads contributed substantially to changes in wheel design, new frame designs, and the develop-ment of pneumatic tires. Furthermore, along with the legal prohibitions on riding, the road problem fostered a commitment among the bicycle's propo-nents take action for political change. Col. Albert Pope and the L.A.W. he founded, for example, were no doubt concerned that whatever investments or technical innovations bicycle manufacturing might have made in moving toward mass production in the 1880s and 1890s, they would have been moot if users could not ride on smooth roads and if laws prevented them from using streets and roads in the first place.

What happened with the bicycle is what historians and philosophers of technology call "stabilization" and "closure" (Bjiker 1995; Rosen 2002). What this means is that early in its history, the specific designs and components associated with a technology can move in multiple possible directions, but this period of relative openness and flexibility begins to close and solidify as important social, political, and economic structures begin forming around a particular technology or design (Rosen 2002: 13). So in the case of the safety bicycle, as manufacturers and investors made important financial outlays in certain kinds of machinery and standardized production processes; as laborers began to organize into industrial worker unions in bicycle factories; as upper and middle class people latched on to the bicycle as a way to show their social distinction and progressive modern attitudes; as women began appropriating the bicycle and influential suffrage leaders connected it to their claims for political and social rights; as a network of repair shops became established; as legal institutions began getting involved in regulating bicycle use; and so on, bicycle technology began to stabilize and close around the design and componentry of the safety bicycle. The idea here is that if none of these forces existed, or had aligned differently, the development of bicycle technology could have gone on a different trajectory.

These processes of stabilization and closure can happen quickly, as they did with the safety bicycle during the 1880s and 1890s, but it does not mean that all avenues of divergent development are necessarily closed automatically. It is possible to see this in the intersection between bicycle technology and the development of motorcycles and automobiles around the beginning of the twentieth century. Human-powered cycle designs and manufacture were not immediately displaced by the manufacture of motorized vehicles. In fact, the lines between motorized and human-powered vehicles were fluid for several decades. Beginning in the 1890s, bicycle mechanics and manufacturers had already begun experimenting with putting internal combustion engines on bicycles, and motorized bicycles became common pace-setting vehicles in bicycle racing (Hurst 2009). At the same time, and continuing well into the twentieth century in Europe, major bicycle manufacturers like Singer, Humber, Rover, and Triumph in England, and Peugeot in France, produced many types of motorized and human-powered vehicles (Cox and Van De Walle 2007: 116–117). They also experimented with different vehicle designs, including tricycles and quadricycles, some of which had motors. One French company called Mochet produced human-powered cyclecars ("velomobiles") in significant numbers during the 1920s and early 1930s, in both single and two-seated versions (Cox and Van De Walle 2007). That many of these human-powered cyclecars were based on recumbent seating positions, or had more than two wheels, suggests that human-powered cycling technology had multiple viable forms (Wilson 2004).

Given that cyclecar and velomobile designs provide more comfort, efficiency, speed, and stability than the safety bicycle, why did these designs not replace the safety bicycle? Certainly, contemporary proponents of the velomobile argue that it should have, and it is possible to argue that a "survival of the fittest" evolutionary narrative would have predicted it. In looking for answers to this question, it is helpful to identify the social, political, and economic structures that might have facilitated or prevented these processes. Some bicycle historians point to a critical decision the main bicycle racing organization, the International Cycling Union, made in 1934 under pressure from powerful elements in the bicycle industry to outlaw recumbent bicycles from racing (because they kept winning) and to enforce a stricter definition of the bicycle around the diamond-frame design we know today (Wilson 2004; Cox and Van De Walle 2007). From that point forward, it made little economic sense for those manufacturers still making recumbent designs to continue producing them, because manufacturers understood well the social and economic prestige of producing successful racing bicycles. And for the most part, recumbent bicycles since then have been relegated to the margins of mainstream bicycle technology. These processes that narrowed the range of technological possibilities for the bicycles were also bolstered by cultural meanings, as explored in Box 2.1.

Box 2.1 Whence the Tricycle?

Most Americans and Europeans are accustomed to thinking of tricycles as appropriate for the extreme ends of life, as an object for the precocious toddler not yet able to ride a bicycle or for the elderly retiree no longer able to ride one. Yet tricycle designs have enjoyed periodic moments of prominence as human-powered vehicles due to their stability, comfort, and practicality for carrying things—and in today's velomobile crowd, tricycle designs are enjoying great respect. So if they're so useful, why doesn't everyone ride one? One answer, as just articulated, has to do with dynamics like the decision in the racing community to outlaw non-diamond-framed bicycles in the twentieth century, which influenced manufacturers to stop experimenting with different designs.

Another answer focuses on the particular cultural meanings associated with both bicycles and tricycles that placed higher symbolic value on bicycle riding, the origins of which go back to the era of the high-wheeler. As the sport of cycling was catching on during the 1870s, tricycles enjoyed growing popularity among children and adults because they required no skill to master, hardly ever tipped over, and provided ladies in particular with a platform to enjoy leisure and exercise without the need for special clothing (Herlihy 2004; Norcliffe 2007). Manufacturers had neglected them previous to the 1870s—bicycles had already gained a reputation as cheaper to build, faster, easier to store, and easier to steer than the few tricycle designs that existed—but with improvements in chain and gear design and increasing use of lighter weight materials, a number of manufacturers—including James Starley of high-wheeler and safety bicycle fame—began producing them in greater numbers.

Figure 2.8 **Tricycle Built for Two.**
Credit: SuperStock

By the late 1870s, tricycles were being used as delivery vehicles and for touring the countryside, and since they were more expensive than bicycles they had snob appeal for socio-economic elites, including the British Royal family. As Herlihy (2004) reports, British newspapers were heralding the coming age of the tricycle and predicting a rosy future. By the 1890s the development of the safety bicycle put a major dampener on enthusiasm for tricycles, however, as one of the biggest justifications—the contrast in riskiness they presented in comparison with the high-wheeler—evaporated. As bicycle manufacturers shifted their attention to safety bicycle technology and the various technical, social, economic, and political processes of stabilization and closure coalesced around the safety bicycle, the tricycle began losing its prominence.

Underpinning these changes was also a new and powerful set of cultural meanings that assigned greater symbolic prestige to the bicycle in the category of "sportiness," since it enabled greater speed and required greater bodily control, balance, and agility on the part of the rider. To be able to ride a bicycle demonstrated qualities of control and mastery over one's body and machine, endowing the rider with social distinction as progressive and modern, qualities that no tricycle rider could claim (Carstensen and Ebert 2012: 26). These days, of course, being able to ride a bicycle carries none of these connotations, but the basic idea of the superiority of the bicycle over the tricycle persists, rooted primarily in the symbolism attached to tricycles, that they are for those who do not have the bodily strength, agility, and control to ride a bicycle.

The broader point here is that saying bicycle design and technology *stabilized* around the safety bicycle in the late nineteenth century is not the same as saying that innovations in bicycle design and other human-powered cycle technology did not take place throughout the twentieth or twenty-first. Over the course of the past century, the bicycle industry has (although not always consistently) been a site of technological experimentation as specific frame designs, frame materials, componentry, gearing systems, and so on have come, and, in plenty of instances, gone. Reflecting this dynamism, in fact, there's an old saying I've heard on multiple occasions doing fieldwork among bicycle enthusiasts that goes this way: "*Question*—When was the bicycle invented? *Answer*—Yesterday." From within the industry it is not unusual to hear something similar, such as the U.S. National Bicycle Dealers Association (2010) which observes that since the 1970s, "no part of the bicycle has remained unchanged, with fundamental improvements in design and materials being the norm throughout the industry."

None of these observations is intended to invalidate conventional histories of the bicycle, such as the version sketched out above that "begins" with the velocipede and "ends" with the safety bicycle. Even though the way this narrative is framed may be problematic, these accounts still offer fascinating and important historical details about the bicycle's origins and the many social and technological changes in which they were involved. Further, these details demonstrate with clarity a point that is central in answering the question this chapter poses, what is a bicycle? Given the historical details laid out above, the answer to this question is clearly that it depends on the *when* of the bicycle, that is, the specific historical moments in which particular shapes or designs have gained socio-technical stability and closure. But at the same time, it is necessary to appreciate the cultural assumptions that shape how North Americans and Europeans think about technological change more generally. In a culture that celebrates technological advancement as an inevitable and good thing, it is easy to dismiss the bicycle as a serious urban mobility option based on the idea that it is technologically stagnant, primitive, and obsolete. This kind of evolutionary thinking can have a disruptive effect on conversations about using bicycles for everyday mobility because it automatically places bicycling on an inferior, almost abnormal and childish plane, and reinforces automobiles and driving a motorized vehicle as the adult norm.

Part Two: A Bicycle is a Multidimensional Object

As much as bicycles and our ways of thinking about them are rooted in particular histories of social and technological transformation, bicycle riders today tend to be unaware of these histories and instead encounter the bicycle as a material object with multiple experiential, individual, social, and political-economic dimensions. It is through these multiple dimensions that bicycles can be said to have "social lives," which is to say, forms, uses, and trajectories that are intertwined in complex ways with people's lives (Appadurai 1986). The full significance of what a bicycle is requires attention to these intersections of human and machine, five of which are especially important for developing an anthropological perspective on the bicycle.[2]

1. A Bicycle Is a Physical Thing

In a most basic sense, a bicycle is a three-dimensional thing that possesses length, width, and depth. It is easy to take these aspects for granted in *any* object, but when it comes to the bicycle in particular, how these three dimensions relate to the person mounting one can hardly be taken for granted. Picture an adult on a child's bicycle or a child on an adult bicycle. If the legs are too short to reach the pedals, or the legs or torso so long that they hit the handlebars, riding a bicycle is impractical, uncomfortable, or downright impossible. As a result since the early days of boneshakers, high-wheelers, and safety bicycles, manufacturers have produced different frame sizes and integrated adjustability to components such as seats and handlebars. Even today among producers, retailers, and dedicated cyclists the issue of "proper fit"—frame sizing (height and length) and the laborious micro-adjustments necessary to align the particularities of one's body with a bicycle and its components—is a major topic of concern (Brown n.d.). Although not everyone agrees on the actual theories and strategies for achieving it, "proper fit" can prevent injuries, ensure a comfortable ride, and maximize performance.

The physical materials from which a bicycle is constructed can also shape a rider's experience of comfort and performance. Modern bicycle frames consist of multiple hollow tubes joined together to create the diamond shape, and although the design has dominated for over a century, there have been numerous innovations during the past two decades in the materials used to make frames and forks (Brightspoke 2011). Depending on the specific material used—which could be an alloy of steel or aluminum, carbon fiber, or titanium—the weight, strength, and stiffness of a frame or fork differ, generating subtle impacts on performance and comfort recognized by experienced riders. Bicycles, of course, include parts made of other materials, such as rubber, plastics, and iron, each of which behaves in different ways given temperatures and other stressors (Ryan and Durning 1997). Other physical factors can also impact performance, such as gearing or something as simple as the width or air pressure of a tire. In addition, accessories added to a bicycle—in the case of the everyday urban cyclist, these might be fenders for keeping road spray off one's clothing, lights for seeing and being seen, racks for carrying things, and so on—can contribute functionality, but they also add weight, wind resistance, and other physical properties that can slow a rider down.

It is not just people who perform on bicycles, however. Bicycles also perform on people, by extending the efficiency of human muscular action and energy expenditure in specific ways, as well as constraining their movements and requiring particular kinds of skills and bodily actions to ride them (Pels et al. 2002: 13; Wilson 2004). These matters involve basic physics, including force, motion, gravity, friction, and inertia (Jones 1970). Consider the dynamics involved in balancing a bicycle. As a "single-track vehicle" (the wheels are on the same line), a bicycle can remain upright (under most circumstances) only while moving. Stability comes from frame geometry, mass distribution, and the gyroscopic effects of spinning wheels (Jones 1970; Wilson 2004). Maintaining balance on a bicycle without falling, especially when turning or leaning, involves momentarily steering in the opposite direction. Riders develop this technique of countersteering, which is often so subtle as to be unnoticeable, as a motor skill based in "procedural memory" (those memory processes that do not involve conscious control), which is why it is said that once learned, bicycle riding is a skill not easily forgotten. In adapting to the physical requirements of the bicycle, a rider's body has to make numerous adjustments most of which do not rise to the surface of consciousness. What *does* rise to consciousness, however, are the sensations the bicycle elicits as it extends a rider's locomotive capabilities and interacts with the ground: the sensation of speed, the burning of lungs, wind in the hair, pain or fatigue in the legs, a sense of fear or exhilaration or mastery, all of which are directly related to the physics of bicycle riding, a bicycle's physical properties, and the interactions between bicycle and environment.

2. A Bicycle Is a Thing With a Past, Present, and Future

In addition to its physical dimensions, a bicycle also has temporal dimensions. That is, each individual bicycle has a past, present, and future connected to its production, exchange, use, and eventual discarding. These temporal dimensions can be productively understood through two lenses, one of these being the idea of an assemblage, a concept that also has bearing on the question of "when" of a bicycle. Standing by itself at a bike rack or in a garage, a bicycle is a physical object that is only partially realized. Once somebody mounts it, the bicycle (not to mention its rider) is transformed into a temporary assemblage (or assembly of human and technology), generating new potential, meaning, and action in the bicycle. The idea here is that the meaning and potential of a bicycle are contingent—that is dependent and conditional—on its temporary use and expression by its involvement with a human. Without the human rider, the object is not yet fully a bicycle.

The other useful temporal lens here is through the notion of a "cultural biography of a thing." As anthropologist Igor Kopytoff (1986: 66–67) observed in his now classic article of the same title, things, like people, follow a life course and it is possible to ask: Where does the thing come from, and who made it? What has it been its career so far, and what do people consider to be an ideal career for such things? What are the recognized periods in the thing's life? How does the thing's use change with age, and what happens when the thing reaches the end of its usefulness?

As Kopytoff explained, biographies of things can facilitate holistic under-standing about issues that might otherwise remain obscure, especially details about the social relationships and cultural ideologies that influence how people create things, exchange them with other people, and use those things in their everyday lives. Across cultures, these relationships and ideologies can vary sub-stantially. For example, the biography of a car (the example Kopytoff uses) in rural Africa would yield very different insights than that of a car in a middle-class North American household because of differences in how the car got there, what it took to purchase it, how and when it gets used and for what, and the specific meanings people make of the automobile itself. In the next chapter I explore how such cross-cultural contexts might impact trajectories of bicycle use. But even within the U.S., bicycles develop distinct biographies related to what kind of bicycle it is (a road racing bike, for example, is likely to have a dif-ferent "career" than a bicycle for everyday urban use) and social factors like the income level, gender, or ethnicity of its users.

To actually undertake a biography of a specific bicycle is a daunting challenge, however, and I don't intend to do it here. It requires going back to the origins of a bicycle's many dozens of parts as raw materials, following these materials through their manufacture and assembly into a bicycle, to the process of that bicycle's distribution and sale as well as its use by an individual or multiple individuals as it changes hands through resale, borrowing, or stealing, and then following what happens after the bicycle is no longer rideable. As you'll see if you try the activity in Box 2.2, to address even the basics of where a bicycle was made and who made it is difficult enough. Why is it so difficult?

Box 2.2 Constructing a Biography of a Bicycle

A bicycle is the tangible product of geographically dispersed transnational capitalist relations. It is also an object that you (and perhaps previous owners) have imprinted on through customization and particular histories of personal use. Constructing a biography of a bicycle is an effective strategy that can help you understand the complex travels of a bicycle through the global economy, illuminating the economic, cultural, and political relationships that enable and shape how an individual might think about, obtain, and use a bicycle.

Opportunity for Reflection and Action

Obtain a bicycle (your own or a friend's), choose three of its components—such as the frame, tires, rims, derailleur, or some other component—and research the following for each component:

- Where did the raw materials come from to make the component and how were they extracted or grown?
- Who manufactured them into finished products?
- How did they get to the place they were purchased by you or someone else?
- What are the intended uses of these components?
- What happens to them after they are used by you or others?

Next, looking at the overall bicycle, try to reconstruct its individual use history, asking:

- How did the bicycle come to your possession?
- What unique markings, scratches, stickers, etc. on the bicycle itself exist, and what might these indicate about the bicycle's history, how it's been used, or specific characteristics of its user(s)?
- What specific meanings and uses does this bicycle hold for you and/or previous owners?

So, how is it possible to find these things out? Begin with a long and close examination of the bicycle itself, as well as the individual components you choose to research. Take notes on any markings, scratches, stickers, or other features that might give clues to the questions raised above. If it's not your bicycle, interview its owner about the bicycle's history with that person. Consult the user's manual, which can sometimes reveal useful information about the origins of the bicycle and its parts. Manuals often come with a new bicycle or component, and if it's a recent model, it is often possible to find one on the company's website. Call a company's customer service line, which can be revealing. Seek out the retailer where the bicycle or components were purchased and conduct an interview about how the bicycle or components came to that shop. Search the internet for the bicycle or component brand name and more general topics such as "where was my bike made?" (you may want to go directly to the following interesting website: http://thebikestand.com/who-made-my-bike.html).

In addition to describing these two distinct aspects of the bicycle's biography, reflect on these bigger questions: In what ways do the transnational and the individual intersect in shaping this bicycle's biography? What was easy about constructing this biography, and what was difficult? Why were some things easy and others difficult? Did any surprising insights emerge for you in this process?

3. A Bicycle Is a Commodity that Circulates Through Complex Political-Economic Relationships

One of the primary reasons for the difficulty of constructing a bicycle's biography comes from the fact that bicycles are mass-produced commodities that circulate globally during their lifetimes, mediating complex political-economic relationships between producers, laborers, and consumers. As Adam Smith observed in his classic work of modern economics *The Wealth of Nations* (1776/1976), the production of goods in capitalism is based on a division of labor that involves "the joint labour of a great multitude of workmen." Citing the example of a woolen coat, Smith listed dozens of *dramatis personae*, from the shepherd and wool-comber to the weaver, merchants, sailors, sail-makers, boat builders, and many others, whose labor either directly or indirectly facilitates a woolen coat's production, distribution, and sale.

But figuring out today where a bicycle comes from and who made it is different than it was in the bygone era of Smith's woolen coat, or, for that matter just several decades ago. Until the 1970s, most of the actors participating directly in the making of a bicycle were concentrated in a single location. You could go to the Schwinn factory in Chicago or the Raleigh factory in Nottingham

(England), for example, where American or British laborers working for an American or British company designed bicycles and drafted blueprints, processed raw materials sourced mostly from that country, crafted and machined the frames and components, assembled those components into bicycles, and then packed those bicycles for shipping to retailers, most of whom were in the same country (Rosen 2002).

By the 1980s, this form of mass production was supplanted by a new style of manufacturing based on globally dispersed networks of suppliers, manufacturers, and distributors distantly removed from the markets in which those goods are sold. Across the European and American bicycle industries, companies were reorganized and began subcontracting out bicycle production to factories in newly industrialized Pacific Rim countries, especially Taiwan and China (Rosen 2002; Witte 2004). As a result of this offshoring, today 99 percent of the bicycles sold in the U.S. are imported from China or Taiwan (NBDA 2010), and approximately two thirds of the 130 million bicycles produced globally each year are made in Chinese factories (Panday 2009). The concentration of bicycle manufacturing facilities in Asia is so great that dozens of the 150 or so bicycle brands sold in the U.S. and Europe are actually made in the very same factories by the same laborers. Some of these brands are examples of "remote control manufacturing," in which a merchanizer based in the U.S. or Europe chooses a bicycle design and componentry from a factory catalogue, places an order, and does little else but affix its own logo on the finished bicycle after it arrives from the factory (Rosen 2002).

Importantly, these Chinese and Taiwanese factories themselves outsource various manufacturing processes to many other suppliers, whose own supply chains, factories, and workshops are themselves dispersed across numerous countries. One of these major suppliers is the Japanese company Shimano, for example, whose own factories are dispersed across Japan, Singapore, Malaysia, and Korea (Rosen 2002). The actual laborers who work in these factories and workshops, processing the metals and plastics, machining them into components, welding frames, and assembling bicycles—not to mention the owners of the transnational firms, holding companies, and conglomerates that manage and receive the bulk of the profits from these processes (Rosen 2002)—are scattered, difficult to trace, and, especially in the case of the owners, sometimes purposefully vague about their role in these processes.

One consequence of this dispersion is that representatives of numerous U.S.-based bicycle companies and retailers I've interviewed are uncertain of the specific origins of the bicycles they sell beyond what the "Made In (name the country)" sticker on the frame says. But these stickers do not necessarily help matters. A typical rule of thumb in the bicycle industry is that the country claiming origin has to add 60 percent or more of the value of the final product

(Roberts 2008). A typical scenario might go something like this: a $1,000 bicycle has a $200 frame and fork manufactured in a Taiwanese factory, which were shipped to Italy where they were painted and assembled for $300 by people who work for a company owned by American and British investors, with $500 worth of components and parts drawn from France, Germany, the U.S., Malaysia, and Japan, then boxed and shipped to the U.S. where it is sold. This bicycle will carry a sticker that says "Made in Italy," but was it really?

The globalized origins and travels of a contemporary mass-produced bicycle are of little concern to most people who buy or ride bicycles here in the U.S., and most remain unaware of the intensive social cooperation and human effort required to make bicycles available for sale, as well as the mostly hidden impacts of bicycle-related industrialization on the lives of anonymous laborers and landscapes in distant places. One explanation for this situation came from another classic analysis of capitalism, Karl Marx's *Das Kapital* (1867/1976), which argued that capitalism breeds a distorted understanding of these cooperative and exploitative relationships. According to Marx, capitalism orients people's attention toward commodities and their trading values, instead of valuing the labor that went into them or recognizing their value as useful things. The result is that commodities exercise a kind of mystical power over people, becoming fetishes of desire and worship. For Marx, that mystical fetish power was intrinsic to commodities themselves, but it must be said that the bicycle industry, perhaps based on the notion that nothing should be left to chance, works hard to cultivate the desire and worship of bicycles.

4. A Bicycle Is an Object of Cultivated Desire

Purchasing a new bicycle is a consequential decision, one that most people who own a bicycle make at most only several times in a lifetime. In the U.S., the cost of a new adult bicycle can range from as little as $150 to more than $10,000, with the average expenditure being in the $300–$500 range (NBDA 2010). About 75 percent of the 15–20 million new bicycles sold each year are low-cost bicycles sold through mass merchants, mainly department, discount, and chain stores like Walmart. Another 15 percent are sold through 4,200 specialty bicycle shops around the country. The remainder of sales is shared between sporting goods stores, specialty outdoor retailers, and the internet (NBDA 2010; Formosa 2011). Individual retailers typically specialize in certain brands (usually around five) and certain styles of bicycles, such as road bikes, mountain bikes, commuter/city bikes, comfort bikes, cruisers, or kids' bikes (NBDA 2010). With the help of bicycle manufacturers, marketing consultants, magazines, newspapers, and the internet, retailers use distinct advertising strategies to draw in customers they want to target. Product placement, juxtapositions between accessories, seasonal discounts and specials, and specialized training of sales staff are all meant to convince those customers to buy something—*anything*—once they get in the store (Bicycle Retailer 2011). Selling new bicycles, in fact, tends to generate insignificant profits for retailers; the real money comes primarily from selling parts, accessories, and service.

Since the late nineteenth century, bicycle peddlers have considered the cultivation of desire for bikes and accessories to be critical to the industry's success. In fact, the bicycle was the first durable luxury item to be mass marketed, and along with the kinds of technical innovations in manufacturing discussed above, during the 1890s the bicycle industry had influential impacts on the rise of modern mass marketing techniques (Petty 1995; Garvey 1996). For example, producers and retailers blanketed newspapers with advertising (10 percent of newspaper advertisements were bicycle-related during the mid 1890s), and advertised heavily in the "new media" of their day, magazines, helping to usher in a new era of advertiser-financed (as opposed to subscriber-financed) media (Petty 1995.). The leading illustrators and artists (including Maxfield Parrish) were hired to paint posters and ads emphasizing imagery of effortless speed, lightness, flight, electricity, the "new woman," and the superiority of the bicycle to other modes of transportation (especially horses and trains) (Figure 2.9). The emphasis in these illustrations was on identifying bicycles with emotionally powerful imagery and as objects of aesthetic appreciation to provoke an irrational desire for the bicycle. These ads also targeted their appeals to discrete segments of the market, by gender, price, lifestyle, and usage (Petty 1995; Garvey 1996). Both of these practices—selling through emotional appeal and market segmentation—remain important strategies in bicycle marketing, and are as likely to travel through our "new media" channels of today, such as Facebook, YouTube, and other online environments.

Throughout its history, the bicycle industry also developed and employed influential techniques of promotion, many of which also remain common today. Key among these were, as Col. Pope once did, contributing to the formation of clubs, bicycle-related publications, and political lobbying groups like the L.A.W. (which eventually changed its name to the League of American Bicyclists, an organization that still enjoys substantial support from manufacturers). To raise the profile of their goods, the industry paid celebrities and famous athletes to appear in their ads and use their products, a form of rider sponsorship that continues today. It also developed the practice of the "annual trade show," the first being held in Springfield, Massachusetts in 1883 (Petty 1995). What drew people to the annual trade show (and continues to do so with Interbike, the most important annual bicycle trade show in the U.S. today) was the introduction of new models and accessories. With the annual trade show, the industry showed that it had adopted the practice of "planned obsolescence," which refers to designing a product to become unfashionable or no longer

Figure 2.9 **Rover Bicycle Catalogue with "New Woman."**
Credit: AIDEA/G. DAGLI ORTI

functional after a certain period, thus stimulating future sales as people return to buy again. though planned obsolescence did not originate with the bicycle industry, its innovation was to introduce a new model every year based largely on stylistic and aesthetic changes (of decoration and paint color, for example) instead of changes of technological substance, which a number of industries (the automobile industry, for one) follow today (Petty 1995).

An exceedingly small minority of bicycle riders or buyers are likely to actually attend an annual trade show like Interbike where the year's new models are displayed with a lot of hype, or even to pay close attention to bicycle ads that appear in magazines or the internet. But they are nevertheless still exposed to longstanding techniques and promotional logic when they buy a bicycle magazine (which features "new products" and has "annual buyers' guides" touting the latest models), view ads in which Lance Armstrong is pushing some product, or enter a bicycle retail environment where bicycles are laid out to feature the newest models in the front of the store, with last year's discounted models semi-hidden in the back even when the differences between them are minimal.

It has to be said also that the manner in which bicycles have been sold in the U.S. has contributed to, and helped sustain, dominant American attitudes toward bicycles as children's toys and as sporting goods. Although only 12 percent of bicycles sold in the U.S. are in the "youth" category (NBDA 2010), for much of the twentieth century the American bicycle industry's primary market was in children's bicycles, and so accordingly its marketing emphasized the idea that they were not meant for adults. Similarly, since the 1970s, the sale of ten-speeds and subsequently mountain bikes was based on marketing the sporting and recreational potential of bicycling. This situation has created a set of conflicting agendas in the selling of cycling, and these agendas have undermined our recognition of bicycles' potential for everyday mobility (Cox 2006). Nevertheless in the past five years or so, the industry has begun marketing images and goods in U.S. markets that emphasize practical everyday purposes, indicating some shifts in bicycle consumer culture. In Box 2.3, I elaborate on what these dynamics suggest for thinking about the relationship between bicycles and consumer culture.

Box 2.3 Bicycles, Cultures of Consumption, and Shopping

Marketing, advertising, and promotion are key elements in contemporary "cultures of consumption," a term that refers to the cultural perspectives, ideas, and activities that shape, and are shaped by, how goods and services are bought and used (McCracken 1988). These processes lie at the heart of consumer cultures because they help construct consumer fantasies, wants, and needs (Grafton-Small 1987). There is more to cultures of consumption than these processes alone, however, which also includes what people actually do with things in their possession and the issue focused on here, how they acquire objects through activities like shopping, arguably a central activity of Americans' everyday lives.

Walking into a store or going online to shop for bicycles and accessories, it is easy to be overwhelmed by the sheer number and variety of possible choices for outfitting oneself and a bicycle, a condition that is not unlike going to a supermarket and finding 15 varieties of cat food. This situation of abundance is somewhat new historically—it emerged in the 1980s and 1990s, when the bicycle industry expanded its offerings during a broader (and ongoing) consumption boom in the U.S. and Europe all of which was fueled by cheap imports from Asia—and from a global point of view, exists in only a handful of wealthy Western countries. Of course, the level of abundance and selection also differs according to the type of store one has entered—at a mass retailer like Walmart the selection is likely to be more limited and low-end than it would be in a typical bicycle retail shop.

Nevertheless, the conventional view of shopping in any of these places is that what shoppers do is a matter of individual choice, reflecting an internal framework of desire or a cost–benefit economic logic that shapes decision-making (Carrier 2004). From an anthropological perspective, such a view of shopping oversimplifies what is really going on. Shopping is a good example of a situation in which peoples' perceptions and practices are both a product of, and help shape the material and social constraints of, their situations (Miller 1987). That is, shopping is only partly a matter of what people like, can afford, or can get access to, as it also involves matters of relationship, identity, social positioning, and the creation of cultural meaning. For example, where and how people shop reflects their desire to associate with certain lifestyles or groups, as well as their dissociation from others (Douglas and Isherwood 1979; Miller 1998a). Shopping also involves relationships of kinship and affection, as individuals shop for and with their families and friends, and consider the effects of their decisions on those close to them—indeed shopping is often viewed as an expression of familial love in the industrialized West (Miller 1998a). Although shopping environments are highly manipulated to get people to buy (Underhill 2004), shoppers are not simply dupes. They exercise agency and creativity as they search for deals, engage in negotiations, and marshal knowledge—which can be closely related to the creation of an individual identity such as "savvy" or "frugal" (Miller 1998). And shopping has moral dimensions, as individuals consider their values and the consequences of their consumption on the environment, the social welfare of workers, the economy, and other concerns (Miller 2001).

Along with emotions like pleasure, shopping often elicits moral tensions and anguish as people realize they're participating in an arena of consumption in ways that contradict their own identities. Such was the case of an environmentalist friend who invited me to go shopping for a bicycle that she could ride to and from work several times a week instead of driving her car. After laboriously choosing a new bicycle that fit her budget and her intended uses—she even considered a used bicycle to lessen the environmental impacts of her purchase—the salesperson presented my friend with many options for customization, including fenders, lights, racks, bags, tools, etc., which led to new rounds of laborious decision-making. As we left with her new bicycle she said, "I feel like I've been barraged. All I wanted was a bicycle. To simplify my life! And here I've got all this other stuff I'm supposed to get. It feels so weird." What "feels weird" perhaps is the contradiction between the notion that a bicycle is a way to simplify one's life and the reality that the bicycle and its accessories are commodities operating in a realm of commercialism and consumption.

Opportunity for Reflection and Action

There is no more useful place to begin exploring ethnographically the relationship between shopping, culture, and bicycles than in retail environments, including mass retailers like Walmart, sporting goods stores like REI or Dick's Sporting Goods, online sites like Bike Nashbar (www. nashbar.com) or Performance Bike (www.performancebike.com), and your local bicycle shop. Go to one or more of these locations to make observations by yourself, or accompany a friend who is going shopping anyway. You can do this exercise casually—that is, simply go in and observe what's going on—or formally by introducing yourself and seeking permission from a manager or owner. Begin by familiarizing yourself with the space and getting a feel for what is going on there, without taking any notes. Once you are ready, take notes on the following:

- What kinds of bicycle-related objects are available, and not available?
- How is space arranged? Is there a logic to it?
- What kinds of behaviors do workers exhibit? Customers? How do they interact with each other?
- What is the variety of specific items (i.e., bicycles, tires, bells, etc.)?

After you leave, reflect on the following questions:

- Do you see any patterns here in how bicycles are presented?
- Do you see any patterns here in how people use space?
- Do you see any patterns here in how people behave around bicycles?
- Why are certain objects available, and others not?
- What expectations did you have of this place? Were they met? Why or why not?
- What are some possible explanations for some of your observations? (For example, why is there only one brand of clothing, but several brands of bicycle?)

Follow up with an in-depth interview with a friend or customer, asking them to describe their own perspectives and experience.

5. A Bicycle Is a Useful Possession

One of the important things about a bicycle is that its value does not lie simply in its tradeability as a commodity. It is also a useful possession that, at the very least, can help move the person who possesses it from A to B. As a result, bicycles are also rooted in a practical social order that presumes certain physical and social networks and arrangements, which may include roads, streets, laws, regulations, and social institutions that support the use of a bicycle (Pels et al. 2002). Furthermore, at least in Western societies such as the U.S., bicycles are a form of property, and so possessing one confers on its user certain kinds of rights and obligations mediated by legal institutions and moral expectations (Hirsch 2010).

In addition to this practical order, bicycles are also rooted in a symbolic expressive order in which people as individuals and as members of social groups create particular cultural meanings and status hierarchies through the consumption and possession of material things (Douglas and Isherwood 1979; Appadurai 1985; Miller 1998b). As various anthropologists have observed, one of the distinctive features of contemporary life in industrialized consumer societies is how much people construct themselves—and are constructed by others—through their relationships with commodities, using those things to express their economic means, gender identities, aesthetic sensibilities, individual qualities of taste and discernment, and identification with a certain social class or interest group (Bourdieu 1979; Miller 1998b). It is thus useful to think of possessing a bicycle as one avenue through which people develop a sense of self and relationship with others, even striving at times to overcome the opposition between themselves and the objects they possess (Miller 2010). It is striking, for example, how often in my ethnographic research on everyday bicycling in my own city I have encountered people who have developed specific and quite personal relationships with the bicycles they use on a regular basis. A surprising number of people give names to their bicycles; place stickers on them and make other purposeful modifications to display personal values, politics, or aesthetic tastes; are able to tell stories about their bicycles; and use expressive and emotional language to describe their relationships with their bicycles. Even for those who do not do these things, bicycles often carry powerful symbolic meanings as the first major possessions they had as children, possessions that gave them for the first time in their lives feelings of independence and freedom.

One particular interview I had with Eric, a forty-something year-old city employee in Burlington, Vermont who rides his bike regularly to and from work and for errands, captures some of the immediacy of emotions expressed about bicycles. Describing his Schwinn city bike, which is almost as old as he is, he almost apologetically explains, "I make do with what I have . . . It's not quite a clunker, but it's old and finicky, and it has failed on me many times. It's heavy to pedal. I've broken pedals and the derailleur. I don't do enough to keep my bike safe from getting stolen. I want and think I deserve an expensive custom-made city bike!" But, he continues, this old bike has a certain vintage aesthetic charm that fits his personal style, and it also has sentimental value to him because he pulled it out of his family's garage where it sat gathering dust for many years. "And anyway," he remarks, "the money I have right now needs to go elsewhere, not a new custom-built city bike. I have no plans to stop using this bike anytime soon." Although clearly expressing ambivalence about that particular bicycle, it is fair to say that through its possession Eric crafts and expresses himself as a certain kind of individual: frugal, stylish, pragmatic, and sentimental at the same time.

So what is a bicycle? In a number of ways, this chapter has barely scratched the surface of what could be a possibly even more complicated and detailed answer. The fact that our common sense still tells us something different than much of what I've covered in these two sections—that it's really still a straightforward little machine with two wheels, pedals, etc.—tells us less about bicycles, however, than it does about common sense. Common sense allows for a kind of short-hand way of communicating that keeps social life flowing. Could you imagine if every time someone said "Look, there's a bicycle!" the answer that came back was "What do you mean by that?" Sometimes this actually can happen—especially when a bicycle is present in an extraordinary context (riding on an interstate freeway, for example)—but for the most part it doesn't and people are grateful for that.

Yet recognizing the extraordinary in the ordinary is one of the hallmarks of an anthropological approach. The common bicycle has played an uncommon role in shaping late nineteenth-and twentieth-century social lives, especially considering its strong social and technological influence over the rise of the automobile; its role in contributing to modern ideas of effortless speed and independent movement; its role in the emergence of modern mass marketing; or its role in the push for women's rights and clothing reform. Furthermore, there is something quite extraordinary in the complex interplay of physical, experiential, social, political-economic, and cultural dimensions that contribute to the ways bicycles aquire social lives and in turn shape social relations. One of the defining things about being human is that we develop deep and complex relationships with the things we make, and bicycles can clearly demonstrate that point in some highly specific ways.

In the next two chapters it will become clear that dislodging common sense perceptions of bicycles is also a major concern of the contemporary bike movement in the U.S. and elsewhere as it promotes greater use of bicycles in everyday urban mobility. Cultural constructions of bicycles as technologically inferior and bicycle riders as somehow unadult or unserious run deep in the U.S. and a number of other automobile-dominated societies, and have concrete impacts on the political prospects of making room for cyclists on roads and the practical viability of using a bicycle to get around. From the vantage point of bicycle advocates and numerous everyday cyclists, the question "what is a bicycle?" is also a loaded one, since rethinking the bicycle is at the top of their political and social agenda. In the next chapter, we explore how and what bicycles mean in three different cities where bicycling is being taken increasingly seriously as a form of urban mobility.

For Further Exploration

There are numerous written histories of bicycle technology and bicycle social history, but several stand out for their readability. Among them is Herlihy's comprehensive and prize-winning *Bicycle: The History* (http://yalepress.yale. edu/yupbooks/book.asp?isbn=9780300120479), Pridmore and Hurd's coffee-table-style book *The American Bicycle* (http://www.amazon.com/The-American-Bicycle-Jay-Pridmore/dp/0760300372), and Macy's young adult book *Wheels of Change: How Women Rode the Bicycle to Freedom* (see Sue Macy's website for a description of the book as well as links to women's bicycle history websites: http://www.suemacy.com/books).

It is possible to see many historic bicycles online, and the "Pedaling History" museum is a good place to start (http://www.pedalinghistory.com/PHhistory. html), as is the National Bicycle History Archive of America (http://www. nbhaa.com/). My favorite bike shop in Burlington, Vermont, the Old Spokes Home, has a world-class collection of historic bicycles gathered by its owner Glenn Eames, which are available for viewing here: http://oldspokeshome. com/full-museum-image-gallery.

There are a number of resources for understanding the science and physics of bicycling, including David Wilson's standard text *Bicycling Science* (http://mitpress.mit.edu/catalog/item/default.asp?ttype=2&tid=10062). The Exploratorium website has an interactive discussion of bicycling science: http://www.exploratorium.edu/cycling/.

For a fascinating look at how mass-produced bicycles were made at the British manufacturer Raleigh during the mid-twentieth century, see the film produced by the British Film Council, "How a Bicycle is Made" (http://vimeo.com/ 39401575). This video pairs well with Paul Rosen's book *Framing Production: Technology, Culture, and Change in the British Bicycle Industry* (http://mitpress.mit.

edu/catalog/item/default.asp?ttype=2&tid=8790).   A   radically   different
approach to bicycle building can be appreciated here (http://vimeo.
com/43062006), which is an interview with Graham "The Flying Scotsman"
Obree about his efforts to build a bicycle (in his kitchen in Scotland) to break
the world land speed record on a human-powered machine.

Daniel Miller's book *Stuff* (http://www.polity.co.uk/book.asp?ref=9780745644233)
offers accessible anthropological perspectives on the complex relationships
between people, commodities, and things, and pairs well with Robert Penn's highly
readable *It's All About the Bike: The Pursuit of Happiness on Two-Wheels* (http://
www.penguin.co.uk/nf/Book/BookDisplay/0,,9780141043791,00.html),   which
recounts the author's travels around the world to put together the ideal bicycle.
See the corresponding BBC documentary about Penn's efforts—couched within a
broader history of bicycles—*The Ride of My Life*, here: http://www.youtube.com/
watch?v=cj4iu8w5Dys.

3

CONSTRUCTING URBAN BICYCLE CULTURES: PERSPECTIVES ON THREE CITIES

"Traveling by bike allows one to penetrate the world of the city: to be in it, with it, of it; it is to know, with each trip, its organization, its disorganization, its history, its future, its holes, its trash, its parks, its walkways, its channels, its people, its lives."

—Mónica Dávila Valencia, *Etnografía de la Ciudad desde la Bicicleta* (*Ethnography of the City by Bicycle*) 2010: 183

On a late Spring afternoon not long ago, a thirty-year-old ecology graduate student named Zach rode his bike through rush-hour traffic in downtown Burlington, Vermont, and a car driver yelled at him.[1] It happened, he recounted to me, on one of the city's main avenues, a four-lane road with two lanes traveling in each direction, as he was waiting behind a line of cars at a signal to make a left turn. Minutes before, he had been riding in the right lane and, in preparation for a lane change, checked over his shoulder several times and indicated his intentions to move to the left lane by pointing his left arm toward it. After an uneventful lane change, he took his place behind the line of cars waiting to turn at the signal, when a station wagon came up from behind him on the right. As it passed, its young male driver yelled angrily out the window, "Get off the road! Get on the bike path, that's what they're for!"

"What bike path was this guy referring to?" Zach asked me rhetorically. Burlington does have several car-free recreational bike paths, but they are all at least half a mile from downtown, and so irrelevant to Zach at that moment. The street Zach was on has no painted stripes to indicate a bike lane, or any other markings or signs for cyclists. Could it be that Zach had done something wrong? No; he had signaled clearly his intentions to change lanes, didn't cut off anybody, and was waiting his turn at the signal. Under Vermont law and Burlington bicycling ordinance, Zach had the legal right to be on this street and, in fact, had no other alternative since technically he was not allowed to ride on the sidewalk in this part of the city. Did general annoyance at bicycles set this driver off? Zach concluded he would never know, since the driver sped off quickly.

In the annals of traffic stories, this incident seems so fleeting and inconsequential that it barely rates mentioning. But as Zach explained to me, it was still an emotionally jarring reminder to him that others do not share his own conviction that getting around the city by bicycle is right and appropriate. That is odd, perhaps, because bicycles are common in Burlington, which has ranked among the top tier of American cities when it comes to conditions for everyday cycling. The city also ranks high on "best of" lists—most liveable cities, best outdoor towns, healthiest cities, best quality of life, etc.—qualities that are closely associated with opportunities for riding bicycles (Ober 2010).

In fact, expressions of anti-bicyclist sentiment and tense interactions with motorists are considered a routine and inevitable part of the culture of urban bicycle riding in Burlington and other U.S. cities. When bicyclists in Burlington get together, it is not uncommon for them to share stories about being yelled at, cut off, and even clipped by motorists. Beyond Burlington, in cities like Dallas, Texas or Orlando, Florida where conditions for cyclists are known widely as dangerous and difficult, riders tell darker stories of conflicts with motorists, involving physical confrontations, life-altering injuries, and even fatalities. Even as bicycling is often celebrated by some as virtuous, convenient, healthy, and green, throughout the U.S. there is a common perception—if not a casual acceptance—that bicycle-riding in city traffic is risky and that people who do it are crazy, stupid, and asking for trouble. Even when, in most cities, the statistics and actual injury rates for bicyclists (which remain quite low) don't support these conclusions. One consequence is a sense of dissonance, a feeling of inconsistency I have often heard expressed among everyday cyclists, including Zach, as "being punished for doing good."

This sense of dissonance—as well as the particular symbolic associations people make with cycling as "doing good" or the casual hostility that some motorists direct toward cyclists—are not universal or necessary aspects of riding a bike in a city. They are elements of a particular urban "bicycle culture," which refers to the social and political-economic organization, cultural meanings, and actual skills, practices, and norms involved in riding a bicycle through a city. This notion is different from the way bicycle industry advertising, advocates, and some bicycle scholars (i.e., Furness 2010) have been using the phrase recently. In those contexts, "bicycle culture" refers to a realm of creative expression involving bicycles, such as bicycle-related arts and crafts, performances, and public displays of bicycling style and imagery, sometimes with a resistance-oriented political agenda. To the anthropologist, these things sound a lot more like the characteristics of a particular sub-culture; a fully anthropological conception of bicycle culture here is rooted in a holistic perspective on the shared meanings, social structures, and experiences associated with bicycle mobility.

As this chapter will show, a global range of possibilities exists for integrating bicycles into an urban mobility system, possibilities that vary across cities and countries. These variations are closely related to the production of distinctive social dynamics and individual sensations, rhythms, skills, and tacit meanings people associate with the bicycle as an object and bicycling as an activity. As anthropologist Tim Ingold has expressed well, such dynamics of urban mobility are both culturally-mediated and highly individualized. Discussing urban walking, he observes:

> As people, in the course of their everyday lives, make their way by foot around a familiar terrain, so its paths, textures and contours, variable through the seasons, are incorporated into their own embodied capacities of movement, awareness and response . . . [T]hese pedestrian movements thread a tangled network of personalized trails through the landscape itself. Through walking, in short, landscapes are woven into life, and lives are woven into the landscape, in a process that is continuous and never-ending.
>
> (Ingold 2004: 333)

The act of riding a bicycle differs from the act of walking in important respects, of course. But the idea that everyday movement through urban landscapes is woven into lives in contextually specific and personalized ways, in which meaning is created through embodied and sensory engagement with a cityscape, is highly relevant to understanding urban bicycle cultures (see also Spinney 2007).

Drawing on a combination of sources, including ethnographic research and secondary materials (published interviews, blogs, and scholarly literature), this chapter offers perspectives on the construction of bicycle cultures in three different cities on three different continents: Amsterdam, in the Netherlands; Bogotá, Colombia; and Burlington, Vermont. It asks: what kinds of infrastructural, political-economic, and social qualities characterize bicycling in these cities? Who rides in these cities, and what are the ordinary pleasures, perils, meanings, skills, and daily politics involved in riding them? In addressing these questions, the goal is not to exhaustively catalogue all aspects and dimensions of bicycle mobility in each city or even to compare them directly on a point-by-point basis, since I've not conducted ethnographic research in all of these cities and the directly comparable published data available for the three cities is minimal. Rather, the goal here is to characterize through qualitative and historical description and analysis how local bicycle cultures are constructed in relation to patterns of urban history, spatial development, and dynamics of land use; public policies and investments in transportation infrastructure and programs; cultural attitudes toward mobility and urban space; and the daily rhythms and informal perceptions and codes involved in getting around by bicycle on particular roads and streets.

Why focus on these three cities in particular? And why no Asian cities, where rates of everyday cycling in some of them are quite high (but also declining; see Haixiao 2012)? For one, large numbers of people in each of the cities discussed here have made conscious decisions to prioritize bicycle use, and they have been recognized by scholars and advocates for those efforts. The fact that these cities do so in distinct measures and in locally meaningful terms, however, is what is important here; my aim is to characterize the diverse criteria used to judge a city as conducive to everyday bicycle use, as well as to highlight how distinct national, regional, and urban histories and cultures contribute to the construction of everyday cycling cultures and experience. The second reason is more tactical, having something to do with the fact that scholarly literature in English on Asian countries where urban cycling is commonplace is, with some notable exceptions (i.e., Moghaddass 2003; Wang 2011; Haixiao 2012), somewhat scarce. Much of the scholarly and advocacy literature on bicycles and cities is, for better or worse, Eurocentric, but what this means is that Amsterdam (celebrated as the "Bicycle City") is an especially well-documented case study. As a Latin Americanist scholar, I am especially interested in what has been taking place in Bogotá, which has become a widely recognized example of how a rapidly growing and largely poor Third World city can take bicycles seriously. And finally, Burlington, which is of course where I've developed a "street's eye" view of urban bicycling through ethnographic research and personal experience, but being neither especially celebrated nor derided, represents well what a small U.S. city can— and cannot—do to take bicycles seriously. In order to lay a solid foundation on which to consider these case studies, the first section provides an overview of cities, urban form, and mobility systems, and then discusses in more detail some considerations of how bicycles fit into those dynamics.

Urban Form, Mobility Systems, and Bicycles

With over half the world's population now living in cities (a proportion expected to grow in the next century), an increasingly important concern in everyday life and urban politics is the issue of mobility. Not only are many cities around the world struggling with pressures of socio-economic transformation, poverty, inequality, and dynamics such as rapid population growth, but as Jarvis et al. (2001: 2) observe, people are more mobile than ever within their cities: "We have moved into an era where we are not simply concerned with a trip to work and back but with the multiple journeys that have become not just desirable but necessary in order to sustain our lifestyles each and every day. It is not an exaggeration to suggest that much of our life in cities is bound up with issues of how to get somewhere." The consequences of ever greater levels of mobility—as well as how people in any given city deal with it—vary depending on factors like the scale and density of the city; its social and institutional complexity; access people in it have to labor, housing, recreation, and services; particularities of income, class, race, gender and so on. Histories of political and economic transformation play an important role, as do residential segregation and other social exclusions that have shaped a city's social relations and "urban form"; in other words, its spatial organization and built environment (Thorns 2002).

The particular urban form of any city is an articulation of multiple forces, including economic, social, technological, cultural, and ideological (Lawrence and Low 1990; Low 1999). Urban spaces and their design have an important impact on social relations, and the processes of defining these spaces involve "sets of social relations [that] introduce and legitimize ways and forms of life. In such circumstances, space and programme either maintain the status quo, or they can be formulated to express alternative social relationships" (Clarke and Dutton, quoted in Pellow 1999: 278). The demand for mobility, and the intra-urban transportation systems set up to accommodate and shape that demand, offer a unique vantage point from which to observe the organization and normalization of urban form and social life. As urban geographer Tim Hall observes (2003: 92), "Movement in cities is not socially benign" since the systems and technologies that mediate urban mobility reconfigure urban spaces, neighborhoods, and the built environment in powerful ways, with far-reaching consequences for people's social relations, daily patterns of business, leisure and home, health, and quality of life.

The relationship between transportation systems and urban spaces follows certain general patterns in modern cities, although there are important local variations as well as variations along a global North–South axis. In Europe and North America, the modern era of mobility began in cities during their periods of initial expansion (1860s–1920s), where there was a boom in intra-city movement related to increasing migration from rural areas, the concentration of new industrial jobs in cities, the separation of work and residence, and the growth in spaces of leisure and consumption such as parks, sporting complexes, and malls. Newly developed bicycles met some of the demand for this increased movement (especially after the turn of the century among working classes as the cost of bicycles dropped), as did the creation of trolley systems and electric street cars (Hart 2001; Thorns 2002; Hall 2003). By the early twentieth century, with the development of commuter rail, urban trams, and subways, numerous cities—among them London, Paris, and New York City—began to decentralize spatially, developing a star-shaped form as "mass-transit cities" in which the city center became the dominant location of employment and social activity, and residences (upper- and middle-class in particular) began to be dispersed in lower-density suburbs connected by train lines (Hart 2001; Jones 2008). Although rates of automobile ownership were still low, the increasing use of automobiles during the 1920s and 1930s saw city streets increasingly retrofitted, traffic laws redesigned, and some highways built to prioritize motorized transportation, all based on a growing conviction among urban leaders and planners that automobiles represented the future. Although streets often represented the largest proportion of public space in cities, non-motorized transportation options were ever more marginalized or excluded in these visions of the future (Hart 2001; Hall 2003; Jones 2008).[2]

After the Second World War, as the mass motorization of North American and European societies became politically, economically, socially, and technologically entrenched in the automobile, a move away from concentrated to even more dispersed urban forms took root. While European cities and their growing suburbs typically maintained public transportation systems and display a tighter spatial agglomeration in their suburban development, many cities in the U.S. "turned inside out," splaying out over large areas connected by extensive road and freeway networks traveled by private cars (Hall 2003; Troy 2012). Beginning in the 1950s, governments throughout Europe and North America invested heavily in expressway systems that stimulated people to move to newly built suburbs, where land and housing were often plentiful and cheap. Educational, financial, and health services soon followed, beginning a trend—in the U.S. mostly unchecked, in some European settings less so—of increasing urbanization in outer suburbs. In the 1970s and 1980s, changes in the global economy motivated the movement of industrial production from urban centers to offshore factories and the rise of service and information economy sector jobs located increasingly in suburbs. These dynamics have driven the growth—particularly in the U.S.—of "edge cities" (suburban downtowns) with low population densities. Today, most jobs in the United States are located not in traditional city centers, but rather in suburban downtowns and corporate campuses (Hanlon et al. 2010).

Post-industrial core cities throughout Europe and North America became increasingly fragmented by networks of high-speed expressways or were surrounded by outer beltways, while newer edge cities expanded almost exclusively around private automobile use. Along with government, powerful capitalist interests drove these dynamics, including the automobile, steel, petroleum, and construction industries, although the vision of ever-expanding roads and highways did not go uncontested (for example, in the U.S., "freeway revolts" were somewhat common in the 1970s; see Jones 2008; Troy 2012). In the process, the physical character and social life of core cities and their public spaces were fundamentally transformed, the story of those (often low-income and immigrant groups) left behind being what Hall (2003: 94) has described as

"a tale of communities who soak up the noise and pollution of urban expressways that plough through or over them, while they rely on ever more decaying
and restricted public transport systems to get around. . . . It is a tale of . . . dead
local economies, financial abandonment and social exclusion, of being immobile in car-cities." One result of these patterns is that calls for "urban revitalization" have dominated European and U.S. discourses about core cities for
several decades, and perhaps not surprisingly, they often call for reducing the
impacts of automobiles and their infrastructure (Hall 2003).

In the rapidly expanding cities of Asia, Africa, and Latin America, patterns of
urban spatial development and social relations vary somewhat. Growth in many
of these cities—some of them referred to as "mega-cities" given their sizes and
high population densities—is recent and ongoing, as rural migrants escaping
conflict, declining subsistence opportunities in rural areas due to economic
globalization and environmental decline, or attracted by the possibility of
better lives and work, pour into cities. The pressure for economic growth and
the imperative to participate in a globalizing economy are just as strong for
these cities as they are for cities of Europe and North America. But with faster
rates of growth in population than of economic opportunity, many migrants
are forced to occupy expanding slums and squatter settlements where resources
are stressed, access to basic services like water, sanitation, and electricity is non-
existent, and where the informal economy rather than formal employment
provides the main means of livelihood (Thorns 2002).

In Latin America in particular—particularly relevant here, since the Bogotá
example discussed below fits this mold—many large cities have developed as
"divided cities" where the upper and middle classes live spatially segregated
from the poor in fortified residential enclaves and spend much of their lives in
privately controlled environments like malls and country clubs (Caldeira 1999).
Public space has historical importance in Latin American cities as a space of
encounter but in the divided city, to be on a public street is a sign of social class:
the rich circulate in private automobiles, while the rest are on foot, bicycles,
or public transit (Caldeira 1999; Berney 2010). High levels of poverty and
social inequality, weak and limited transportation infrastructure that often does
not reach into slums, and sometimes expensive public bus systems mean that
intra-city mobility options are limited for the social majorities (Thorns 2002;
Brussel and Zuidgeest 2012). At the same time, most of these cities have
undergone rapid and unplanned motorization, becoming traffic-choked and
heavily polluted by a minority of the people who can afford automobiles
(Cervero et al. 2009).

What do these distinct dynamics of urban space and mobility mean for
bicycles? Although bicycles have long been present in most, if not all, of the
world's cities, the majority of them (outside of a relative handful of Asian and

European cities) did not develop spatially or socially around prioritizing mass bicycle use in their transport networks.[3] Further, global trends in the increased motorization of urban mobility and the reorganization of urban spaces to facilitate it have tended toward the marginalization of the bicycle, as well as other forms of non-motorized urban mobility. In the U.S. and Europe, this is especially the case in the suburbs, and in rapidly growing cities in the global South, the quick and mostly unplanned motorization of cities has marginalized the use of bicycles in city centers. Geographic factors such as challenging climates and hilly topography have also had some influence over this trend, although these are hardly determining factors since there are plenty of warm or dry cities where bicycling is minimal, and cold, wet, or hilly places where cycling is more common. More important tend to be urban forms in which distances are too great and urban densities are too low for practical bicycle use; policies that restrict, prevent, or shape perceptions of cycling as unsafe because bicycles are seen to interfere with the efficient movement of motorized vehicles or other forms of high-capacity travel; limited transportation funding investment in anything other than automobiles and public transit; concerns about bicycle costs or high rates of bicycle theft; or insufficient on-road facilities, legal protections, or social support for cycling (Reitveld and Daniel 2004; Parkin 2012; Krizek 2012). All of these reasons are framed and bolstered by culturally powerful ideologies, such as a preference for speed or the notion that bicycles are childish, unadvanced, or vehicles of the poor, some of which were discussed in the previous chapter.

Nevertheless, it is often said that even under many of the conditions discussed above, cities are ideal environments for bicycles, or as one observer (Gardner 1998) has noted: "Bicycles are as natural to urban transport as wildebeest are to the East African savannah or as salmon are to North America's Columbia River." Though such language naturalizes something that is not at all "natural" (because these conditions are manufactured by people), one of the main arguments for this position is closely tied to the relationship between bicycling and urban form: where there is population density and mixed land use patterns in which residential, work, educational, and recreational spaces exist in close proximity to each other, the distances people travel in their everyday lives are often short and bikeable (Gardner 1998; Krizek 2012). In the U.S., for example, 40 percent of trips people take in cities are under two miles and in Great Britain it is 50 percent of trips, both of which are widely considered bikeable distances by a majority of adults surveyed (Gardner 1998). Furthermore, where cars dominate, these same conditions of density tend to create slow-moving traffic and result in congestion. Bicycles offer flexibility, allowing riders to bypass congestion by taking alternative routes such as alleyways and even (when appropriate) sidewalks, and since they take up less space, tend to move through urban traffic efficiently and quickly.[4] Furthermore, 18 to 20 bikes can fit into a single car's parking space, reducing demand on space-intensive and expensive parking facilities.

The greater use of bicycles in the urban transportation mix has also been articulated as an issue of economic rationality. Bicycles operate at a fraction of the cost of motorized vehicles, making them (in theory at least) accessible to a wide variety of socio-economic groups. This is especially the case for those who cannot gain access to automobiles or even public transit due to a lack of financial resources or because buses and the transportation infrastructure do not reach their location. Moreover, as highly efficient vehicles, bicycles can buffer their users from volatile costs associated with petroleum energy markets, which are expected to rise in line with increasing scarcity (Krizek 2012; Troy 2012). Because their impacts on street infrastructure are minimal, bicycles entail lower public expenditures on infrastucture (Pucher and Buehler 2008). They also provide a means to save on public health care costs: urban spatial forms in which people do not walk much and sit for long periods in motorized vehicles contribute to chronic diseases related to a sedentary lifestyle, such as obesity, poor cardiovascular health, and diabetes. Bicycles and other forms of active mobility are thus often presented as a means to improve the health of urban populations (Cervero 2009; Pucher et al. 2010). The health benefits of cycling, in fact, have been shown in most cases to exceed the health risks from traffic injuries, and these risks generally decrease as rates of cycling rise (Pucher et al. 2010; Krizek 2012). Bicycles also offer an alternative to the high environmental costs of motorized transportation, reducing the ecological burdens of motorized vehicles by eliminating noxious emissions and carcinogenic particulate matter that contribute to air and water pollution, both of which negatively impact city-dwellers' health, urban landscapes and waterways, and global climate (Gardner 1998).

Beyond these economic arguments exists another realm of values-based debate. Highlighting their positive impact on well-being, some have asserted that bicycles represent a sharp quality of life contrast with motor vehicles, generating distinctive and positive patterns of urban street life and a better use of limited urban public space. Central to these assertions are ideas associated with Jane Jacobs (1992)—who contended that the greatness of cities lies in the social life of sidewalks and the possibilities for human interaction cities generate—and Austrian philosopher Ivan Illich's (1973) view that on bicycles people can become masters of their own movement without blocking the movements of others. Unlike the anonymity, lack of social accountability, and high speeds associated with automobiles, bicycles can render their users open to social interaction with other urban dwellers, contributing to the creation of quiet, convivial, and equitable urban environments (Illich 1973; Parkin 2012).

Recent efforts to promote bicycles through urban "liveability" initiatives—like the ones in Chicago described in the preface—have often emphasized these factors, as have urban planning frameworks like "the New Urbanism."[5]

One of the big questions and growing controversies in some cities related to this last point, however, is whose urban quality of life is improved through bicycles. A driving force of contemporary urban revitalization and liveability initiatives in which bicycles have played a role is to attract service workers, investment, and tourism, processes that often draw public investment and political attention away from lower-income neighborhoods. As Rutheiser (1999) notes, the logic of urban revitalization initiatives is often focused on revitalizing real estate values or the production of artful designs and architecture, not focused on changing social relations. As a result, in certain low-income and minority neighborhoods in New York City, Washington, D.C., and Portland, Oregon, for example, residents have mounted sharp resistance to urban revitalization programs, viewing them as "code for efforts to drive them out, and the building of dog parks and bike and streetcar lanes as efforts by affluent whites to re-arrange spending priorities to suit themselves" (Tavernise 2011). In certain quarters, bicycles have come to be viewed as "expressways to gentrification," developing a close symbolic association with higher costs of living and the exacerbation of social conflict in neighborhoods where class and racial differences are already tense (DeSena 2009; Davis 2011). In other cases, such as Chicago, bicycles have been embraced by community leaders as one strategy to improve poor public health in deprived and minority neighborhoods, but in fact more resources for bicycle programs and infrastructure have gone to upper- and middle-class sectors of the city (Lepeska 2011).

Still, there has been growing awareness during the past decade among transportation scholars, urban leaders, and at higher levels of government (notably the European Union and U.S. Department of Transportation) that bicycling needs to play a much larger role in urban mobility systems (Pucher and Buehler 2008: 497). Many of the reasons for it were just presented above and are explored in further detail below, but they often align closely with broader political-economic and social agendas, including making transportation systems more ecologically and economically sustainable. This tends to mean that they are less polluting and less energy intensive, as well as more accessible to a wider array of people (Litman 2003; Steg and Gifford 2005; Buehler and Pucher 2010). They are also linked to a public health agenda in which there is growing awareness that urban spatial patterns and the built environment affect people's activity patterns and thus health (Cervero et al. 2009). These agendas are all based on imagining alternatives to an urban status quo, and the bicycle has as a result gained a strong symbolic association as an "alternative" form of urban transport.

Much of the current scholarly research on this view of bicycling concentrates on the specific practical actions and investments that support or improve the safety, convenience, and attractiveness of urban bicycle use (Reitveld and Daniel 2004; Pucher and Buehler 2008; Pucher et al. 2010; Xing et al. 2010; Pucher et al. 2011; Krizek 2012). These studies focus mostly on European, Canadian, and U.S. cities and, reflecting their origins in disciplines like planning and civil engineering, they are largely quantitative and statistical in orientation, drawing from aggregated demographic data sources like censuses, traffic counts, and travel surveys to identify general patterns in rates of cycling as they relate to initiatives specifically implemented to promote cycling. One consensus finding is that cities that achieve high levels of cycling make certain kinds of changes in urban form and the built environment by retrofitting motor vehicle-centric infrastructure to accommodate bicycle riders, particularly by creating infrastructural treatments on streets that separate cyclists from motorists. The most common of these treatments are presented in Box 3.1.

Box 3.1 Common Bicycle Infrastructure Treatments (adapted from Pucher et al. 2010)

On-road bicycle lanes. Painted stripes on the margins of roads. Some lanes might be colored as well.

Cycle tracks. Similar to bike lanes, but they make a physical separation between travel lanes using curbs, vehicle parking, or some other barrier.

Off-street paths. Sometimes called "trails" and often shared with other users, such as walkers. Provide a paved path separate from motor vehicle traffic that allows for two-way bicycle traffic.

Signed bicycle routes. Shared roadways designated with signs as a preferred route for cyclists. Also includes wayfinding signs that include common destinations and the distance or time to get there.

Sharrows. "Share the road" arrows painted on roads that indicate to cyclists and motorists that bicycles share the road.

Special traffic signals for bicycles. Specially timed traffic lights that allow cyclists a head start through intersections.

Bike boxes. Painted areas at a signalized intersection in front of a motor vehicle lane, where cyclists wait until the light changes. Makes cyclists more visible and gives them a head start through an intersection.

Bicycle boulevards. Signed bicycle routes on low-traffic streets, often with traffic-calming measures to slow or discourage motor vehicle traffic.

Contra-flow lanes. Two-way travel on one-way streets, in which bicycles ride in a protected lane against one-way traffic.

Integration of bicycles with public transit. Special racks on buses to hold bicycles; bike parking at public bus or train stations; rail cars; or ferries with bicycle hangers; bicycle rental stations.

End-of-trip facilities. Includes bike parking (bike racks, sheltered/unsheltered bike parking, guarded areas, and bike lockers); showers at workplaces; and bicycle stations (full-service facilities offering bike parking, rentals, repair stations, showers, bicycle washing stations, etc.), which are often located in commercial districts or next to train stations.

Traffic calming techniques. Physical changes in streetscapes that slow motor vehicle traffic, including speed bumps, traffic circles, curb bump-outs, lamp posts, benches, trees, play structures, slow speed limits, physical barriers, and other changes to sidewalks and pavement.

Car-free zones. Neighborhoods closed to cars, or temporary closure of roads to motor vehicle traffic (also called *ciclovías*; see the section on Bogotá).

Opportunities for Reflection and Action

Do an inventory of bicycle infrastructure in your community or your campus. Which of these facilities exist and where are they in relation to the likely points of interest for someone who gets around by bicycle, such as shopping, housing, work, and services? Spend some time observing the ways cyclists use particular infrastructure treatments. Are there variations in how different cyclists use them? What factors, aside from the infrastructure treatment itself, might influence cyclist behaviors and perceptions?

A second conclusion is that these treatments do not work in isolation. The evidence suggests that these treatments need to be systematically incorporated into a comprehensive network of cycling infrastructure, rather than exist as piecemeal efforts. Furthermore, infrastructure change does not on its own appear to support cycling. Mutually reinforcing initiatives are thus common, including the implementation of motor vehicle reduction policies and programs (i.e., increasing car or fuel taxes; "congestion charging," which is charging motorists a fee to enter the city center; etc.); educational, promotional, and incentive programs (i.e., targeted marketing, bicycle skills courses, bicycle give-aways, "bike to work days," street safety awareness campaigns, recreational cycling events, car-free events, financial incentive programs for cyclists, etc.); and legal interventions (helmet laws, speed limits, targeted enforcement, etc.).

These studies, along with other bicycle-related research conducted by transportation engineering and planning scholars, have contributed to a recent surge in knowledge about the relationship between bicycles and cities, at least in the specific conditions of affluent and industrialized Western cities. These scholars continue to debate which treatments and programs give "the best bang for the buck," that is, generate safe and cost-effective increases in rates of cycling (Krizek 2012). But it has to be said that, even while providing practical guidance for urban traffic management and bicycle promotion policies and programs in certain places, much of this research presents a partial and mostly culturally uninformed picture of the relationship between cities, people, and bicycles. With narrowly framed research questions and conclusions derived from statistical analyses of aggregated data sources, the primary outcomes of this research tend to be lists of one-size-fits-all technical treatments and cycling stimulation policies based on a "build-it-and-they-will-come" logic. One can easily get the false impression that material and policy changes alone shape the desire and experience of riding a bicycle in a city, or that bicycles themselves are technologically and symbolically neutral objects. It is possible to forget that cycling is a human activity involving actual people who have diverse and locally situated histories and relationships with cycling and urban spaces, and that bicycles themselves are heterogeneous and contextual objects.

Bicycling *is* highly sensitive to material conditions such as urban spatial form, the built environment, and traffic policy. But it is also highly sensitive to cultural attitudes, symbolic constructions, and social relations (Carstensen and Ebert 2012). These socio-cultural dimensions include the daily manifestations and practices associated with the political-economic and social hierarchies embedded in transportation systems; the meanings and experiences different people project onto and derive from the bicycle itself; choices and individual preferences associated with daily mobility, which are closely tied to perceptions and ideologies about urban space; social norms, expectations, and informal codes about how to ride; and the embodied demands and skill sets involved in navigating city streets. Furthermore, not all cities are created equally: even while there are certain general characteristics that shape the relationship between urban spatial form and a mobility system, there are historical, political-economic, and social particularities to each story that powerfully shape the characteristics of a local bicycling culture. The goal of the next three sections is to explore these dynamics in specific urban contexts, beginning with what many observers consider to offer a "gold standard" for urban bicycling, Amsterdam.

AMSTERDAM: Unfazed and Nonplussed on Two Wheels

On any given day in Amsterdam, the largest city in the Netherlands with a population of 780,000 and the country's capital, streets are filled with people of all ages and income groups going about their daily lives using bicycles (Figure 3.1). It is a city where some 38 percent of trips are made by bicycle, which since 2007 has been higher than the percentage of car trips made there. Although the rate of cycling is actually lower than in some other Dutch cities, Amsterdammers use their bicycles intensively, with half the residents making daily use of a bicycle, mostly for short trips under a couple of kilometers (Buehler and Pucher 2010; Fietsberaad 2010). Almost half of these riders are women, and substantial numbers of riders are elderly. Kids ride too, and it is common to see babies strapped on to bicycle seats. Seventy-three percent of Amsterdammers own a bicycle, and riding one is such a common and unremarkable activity that attitudes toward the act of cycling have been described by a prominent Dutch cycling blogger as "unfazed and nonplussed" (Amsterdamize 2011). Getting around by bicycle is a self-evident routine, making it, according to a Dutch sociologist, "neither a concious lifestyle nor a political statement" (Kuipers 2012: 2). Even as many people cycle, most do not consider themselves to be "cyclists," that is, people who consciously prioritize bicycling as an activity. It is, quite simply, a normal routine of everyday life.

These levels of cycling, as well as its apparent naturalness, are unheard of in any comparably sized European or North American city—perhaps with the exception of Copenhagen, Denmark, which is almost twice as large. Amsterdam has gained a reputation as a kind of Shangri-La for urban bicycling among

Figure 3.1 **Getting Around Amsterdam.**
Credit: fotosol

foreign tourists, bicycle advocates, and bicycle transportation planners, an image the Dutch have projected to the wider world through national branding and tourism advertising (Kuipers 2012). Amsterdam's flat topography and moderate climate are often offered as explanations for why it is such a good place to bicycle. But more significant factors include the city's dense spatial development patterns and mixed-use neighborhoods that make cycling distances short, and its bicycle-specific infrastructure—including 450 km of cycle tracks, bike paths, and bike lanes; two hundred thousand spaces for parking bicycles; and integration of bicycles into the city's public trams and buses—that help make it convenient and speedy (Buehler and Pucher 2010: 38; Reitveld and Daniel 2004; Fietsberaad 2010). There is also a strong perception that it is safe, which has to do with a social hierarchy of mobility in which pedestrians and bicycles, not cars, are given priority in the city's traffic flow. Indeed, when there is an accident, the assumption is that it is the motorist who is at fault, which contributes to a sense of caution among drivers that encourages them to look out for cyclists. The city also greatly restricts the access motorists have to the city center: numerous streets are one-way for cars (but not for cyclists), others are completely off limits to cars, speed limits are low (30 km/hr or about 19 mph), and parking is sparse and costly (Mapes 2009; Buehler and Pucher 2010).

Most of Amsterdam's bicycle infrastructure and policies were implemented after the 1970s, in a reversal of a general decline in cycling in the city. In 1955, 75 percent of trips in Amsterdam were made by bicycle, but this had declined to 25 percent in 1970 (Fietsberaad 2006). After the Second World War, Dutch state and municipal planning were rooted in the belief that bicycles were outdated and inferior, and that progress was based on increasing private car ownership, concentrated decentralization development patterns (building suburban centers), and highway construction projects (Schwanen et al. 2004; Carstensen and Ebert 2012). These changes were not met without resistance in Amsterdam, which had a difficult time coping with the crowding, demolition of buildings, and pollution caused by automobiles. During the mid 1960s, an anti-consumerist youth movement called the Provos famously confronted these challenges by proposing to close Amsterdam to all motorized traffic and to replace automobiles with bicycles. In what is one of the first bike-share programs in the world, they painted 50 bikes white and left them on the streets for free public use (though they were quickly confiscated by police). During the 1970s, the cumulative effect of declining state investments in the inner city and the demolition of affordable housing in order to make way for new buildings and automobile infrastructure were met with popular protests and a squatters' movement, which succeeded in raising issues of community justice and equity in city government (Soja 1992; Uitermark 2009; Furness 2010). New meanings were attached to the bicycle during this period, especially as a way of living anti-capitalist values and pursuing the development of locally oriented cultures.

At the same time, various challenges to the automobile were being mounted at the national level. The Netherlands was hit especially hard by the 1973 oil crisis, which led the government to implement "car-free Sundays" in cities to conserve petrol. A national campaign against "kinder moord" (the murder of children) also steered public concern toward the problem of child deaths in automobile accidents. Politicians responded by introducing policies to strengthen controls and taxes on automobile use, modify city and transportation planning regulations to favor more compact urban development, and provide financial support for increasing bicycle transportation (Schwanen et al. 2004). A key development was the creation in 1975 of a national fund to support the construction of urban and rural bicycle infrastructure (Reitveld and Daniel 2004; Ebert 2004; Fietsberaad 2010). In Amsterdam, a newly elected city council in 1978 made the decision to focus on bicycling as an integral tool for confronting the city's transportation and urban land use problems. This, along with the new interest in promoting bicycles at the national level, made bicycle policy a mainstream political issue (Buehler and Pucher 2010).

The political struggles and eventual mainstreaming of bicycles during the 1970s laid the groundwork for a cycling renaissance during the past 30 years, but the bicycle culture that has emerged was also enabled by a distinctive *Dutch* cycling culture that has long viewed the bicycle as a powerful national symbol (Carstensen and Ebert 2012). This culture has its origins in the 1880s when bicycles were first imported from Great Britain. Although bicycles were viewed skeptically as a foreign technology and, given their expense, limited to urban upper classes, proponents of the bicycle associated with the Dutch Cycling Union (founded in 1883) succeeded in presenting the bicycle as a way to tour the Dutch countryside and a means to unify what was then a fractured country, as well as to promote "traditional" national values of independence, self-confidence, self-control, and consistency which needed to be preserved and reasserted in a changing world (Ebert 2004: 356). The bicycle was symbolized as simple and informal, appealing to notions of status among Dutch social elites, where displays of ostentation were de-emphasized (Kuipers 2012). By the turn of the century, the close identification of the Dutch royal family with bicycles, the rise of a home-grown bicycle industry, and the proliferating use of bicycles among the working classes as bicycles became less expensive helped cement a close association between bicycles and Dutch national identity (Figure 3.2). To be Dutch was to ride a bicycle.

Significantly, the Dutch culture of cycling developed certain particularistic elements, marking it as distinct from cycling cultures in other European

Figure 3.2 **Images of Dutch National Identity.**
Credit: © Barbara Singer

nations. For example, the Dutch Cycling Union rejected racing and heavily emphasized the virtues of bicycle touring and everyday bicycle use.[6] The Union used its influence to help shape the first nation-wide traffic law (passed in 1905) that outlawed bicycle racing on streets, and at the same time recognized bicycles and motor vehicles as the central protagonists of the new era of transportation (Carstensen and Ebert 2012). The social and political legitimacy of the everyday transportational use of bicycles generated some of the highest rates of cycling in Europe throughout the first half of the twentieth century.[7] Furthermore, this view of transportation was not based on antagonism between the automobile and bicycle—both were good for touring, went the thinking—so even decades later as the post-war automobile boom eroded cycling conditions, the basic idea that bicycles had legitimacy on roads and as a form of transportation was ingrained in Dutch planning traditions and the country's national imagination.

Another key dimension of this culture is that, as Dutch sociologist Giselinde Kuipers (2012: 9) offers, "All Dutch are embedded in a network of conventions, habits, and practices to do with cycling that are felt to be self-evident." What are some of these formal and informal conventions, habits, practices, and meanings involved in cycling in Amsterdam?[8] To start with the bicycle itself, Amsterdammers tend to think of bicycles as tools of everyday life, appliances as opposed to sporting goods.[9] Dutch manufacturers developed a common bicycle type during the twentieth century that emphasizes its practicality for everyday use: a sturdy bicycle with wide tires for comfort and durability, an upright seating position with back-swept handlebars, front and rear lights, a skirt guard, fenders, racks, and baskets, among other qualities (Henbrow 2009; Pelzer 2010, see Figure 3.3). In Amsterdam, such bicycles are common, although bicycle types have become more heterogeneous in recent years as manufacturers have created new bicycle types (cargo bikes, folding bikes, mountain bikes, bicycle taxis, etc.), and bicycle and consumer cultures imported from other countries have contributed to changing ideas about desirable bicycle types (Carstensen and Ebert 2012). Nevertheless, the appearance of many bikes is old, practical, and battered, and many people actually prefer it that way, the

Figure 3.3 **Dutch Bikes Parked on Canal Bridge, Amsterdam.**
Credit: © 2009 Getty Images

thinking being that it makes the bicycle unattractive to thieves, bicycle theft being a major issue in the city (Buehler and Pucher 2010).

In explaining why and how they get around on bicycles, Amsterdammers tend to emphasize their speed as a primary factor (Slütter 2012). It is simply faster to get places by bicycle than by car or public transit—both of which are widely considered slow and less convenient, if not also more expensive and more stressful—and this emphasis on speed and convenience has an impact on route choice. Although quiet streets or streets with protected bike lanes are generally considered nice to cycle, priority tends to be placed on the directness of routes (Pelzer 2010). Because the pattern of streets is dense and complicated— the city is not laid out in a grid pattern like many more recently built cities— residents develop particular place-based understandings of which routes are most direct, which intersections are quickest to get through at certain times of day, etc. At the same time, however, an emphasis on homogeneity of design and predictability in Amsterdam's bicycle infrastructure facilitates rapid and convenient movement (Lee 2011).

Since cars are not perceived as a threat and traffic speeds are low, serious accidents are infrequent and helmet use is uncommon, even strenuously rejected because it communicates a wrong impression that cycling is a risky activity (Buehler and Pucher 2010). Cyclists, according to one resident, are conceived as "pedestrians who simply move a bit faster" (Robson 2012), and any threat they represent is mostly to themselves or other cyclists. Nevertheless, the assumption is that bicycle riding requires training, and children receive instruction in urban riding in school. The actual rhythm and flow of bicycle traffic is described by many as one of "organized chaos" (Robson 2012) or a "complicated dance of which everyone knows the steps" (Mapes 2009: 61; Pelzer 2010)—a rhythm that prominent urban theorist, Edward Soja (1992) identified several decades ago, as a broader characteristic of Amsterdam's urban social patterns. Riders tend to be responsive to each other and traffic conditions, as opposed to always following the explicit rules like stop signs and signals. For example, a visiting bicycle advocate from Scotland describes a ride where cyclists around him slowed down but did not stop at red lights, especially where there was no cross-traffic. He decided to go with the flow, which seemed to be what other cyclists were doing. When he decided to stop at a red light, even though there was no cross-traffic, other cyclists coming up behind him stopped as well without any sign of being annoyed or impatient (Robson 2012). Astonished that people don't crash into each other, the Scot asked an Amsterdam friend for an explanation, to which the Amsterdammer replied, "They don't because they grow up biking and never stop. They're skilled and the key thing to their effortlessness is that they're good at anticipating traffic, specially other people on bicycles" (Robson 2012).[10]

It would be mistaken to view Amsterdam's culture of everyday cycling as static, and it is still in formation. Dynamics of globalization, migration, European integration, and polarization within Dutch culture and politics have contributed to ongoing changes in Amsterdam's urban bicycle culture (Kuipers 2012). In recent years, for example, the profile of cyclists has been shifting away from its historically wide socio-economic spectrum. Today, the city's cyclists tend to be highly educated and middle class, while lower-class citizens and especially new immigrants are more likely to get around by automobile (Buehler and Pucher 2010; Fietsberaad 2011; Kuipers 2012). The meanings of bicycles and the activity of cycling are also shifting. No longer do Amsterdammers view cycling as a prototypically unpretentious "Dutch" activity. They are increasingly re-imagining cycling as an activity that is "doing good" for the planet and its residents, which is part of a broader positioning of Amsterdam within Europe as symbol of "urban liveability," a concept that focuses on an ecologically sustainable and social urban environment that offers a rich variety of experiences (Carstensen and Ebert 2012: 48). Bicycle culture in Amsterdam is also becoming visually expressive and more closely tied to international fashion trends, for example in websites that celebrate the stylish and hip fashions of cyclists that ride the streets of the city. The blog Amsterdamize, for example, features glossy photos of well-dressed women and men getting around the city by bicycle. These changes might communicate to the rest of the world that Amsterdammers are at the cutting edge of urban hipness and sustainability, but underlying and intertwined with these changes in perceptions Amsterdammers have about themselves and their city, are deeper histories of Dutch relationships with cycling.

BOGOTÁ: "Bicycle Consciousness" and the Right to the City

Until just over a decade ago, the Colombian capital city of Bogotá was viewed widely—not least by its residents—as one of the worst cities in the world, an urban basket case dominated by chaos, poverty, kidnappings, and violence. To refer to Bogotá as, among other things, a world-class "biking paradise" and at the cutting edge of sustainable urban transportation would have been inconceivable. Yet this Andean city of 7.5 million people has in the past few years gained an international reputation for just these things (Cervero et al. 2009; Wallace 2011). The city's ongoing transformation—in which bicycles and the cultivation of what a recent mayor called "bicycle consciousness" play protagonistic roles—has been shaped by the notion that all residents have a right to the city, and that a commitment to constructing accessible urban mobility and public spaces enables people to exercise that right (Peñalosa 2002; Montezuma 2005; Berney 2010).

One expression of the right to the city that happens every Sunday morning and on most holidays is the city's *ciclovía recreativa* ("recreational bike way") in which 121 kilometers of avenues and streets are closed to automobiles between the hours of 7am and 2pm. These events typically attract about a million people of all ages and income levels—numbers that swell even higher during holidays—who take over the streets for walking, jogging, skateboarding, rollerblading, and riding bicycles.[11] *La Ciclovía*, as it is known, has a festive and relaxed tone (it's sometimes called "the world's longest street party"): individuals and families ramble and socialize, food vendors sell snacks on sidewalks, stations throughout the city provide free bicycle repairs, health information, and other services, and at public parks and squares, free aerobics and dance classes are offered and bicycles are available for free use (Sarmiento et al. 2010; Montes et al. 2011, see Figure 3.4). Residents count *Ciclovía* as one of the most desirable aspects of their city, and it has been widely imitated throughout the Americas (Sarmiento et al. 2010).[12] A complementary expression of the right to the city is the recently built $200 million *Cicloruta* ("Cycle Route"), a 350 kilometer network of dedicated bike lanes and cycle tracks backed by Dutch advisors that provides bicycle riders the ability to move between many of the city's high-density neighborhoods, commercial, and cultural centers while being (mostly) protected from cars. Other bicycle initiatives include bicycle-specific signage, intersection signals, a mandatory helmet law, and thousands of new bicycle racks and parking facilities throughout the city due to a requirement that buildings make bicycle parking available.

Figure 3.4 ***Ciclovía*** **in Bogotá.**
Credit: Krzysztof Dydynski

In these prominent initiatives, bicycles are portrayed as a fun and healthy way to get exercise and a useful and convenient means of getting around the city, ideas that carry a particular resonance among Colombians. Perhaps more so than in many other Latin American countries, Colombians have important historical associations with the bicycle. During much of the past century, bicycle use has been common throughout Colombia, as recreational vehicles in wealthy households and as a common form of transportation among the country's poor (Pardo 2010). Colombians have also identified closely with international bicycle racing, and it vies with soccer as the country's unofficial national sport (Rendell 2003). Since 1950, the country has hosted one of the world's most grueling races, the *Vuelta a Colombia* (Tour of Colombia), and during the past 30 years it has produced some of the world's most competitive and accomplished riders in international racing. Bogotá's *Ciclovía* is also one of the earliest and longest-running car-free events in the world: inaugurated in 1974, it was motivated by Bogotá cyclists protesting a lack of urban recreational opportunities, traffic congestion, and pollution (IDRD n.d.).

Yet in Bogotá, the recreational and everyday use of the bicycle long confronted enormous practical and social challenges associated with the city's patterns of spatial and social development as a "divided city." Since the middle of the twentieth century, Bogotá has experienced staggering growth rates and increases in population density as millions of impoverished rural migrants poured into the city to escape the violence of escalating civil war, drug cartels, and death squads in the countryside. The city was ill-equipped to handle that growth. A number of factors laid the groundwork for the city's urban divide: ineffective city institutions, a mayor appointed by (and beholden to) the country's president, the organization of the city into private residential subdivisions, illegal seizures of public land by private interests, and the self-segregation of the wealthy and middle classes in their own neighborhoods and country clubs (Berney 2010). The results were social and spatial exclusion, inadequate housing options for the poor, the physical fragmentation of the city into distinct sectors, a dearth of public spaces, insecurity and violence, and indifference to civic life.

These historical dynamics had important consequences for urban mobility. Bogotá had developed a small tram system with limited practicality as a form of mass transit in the early twentieth century, and beginning in the 1930s, a privately controlled bus system was developed to carry the city's growing population (Montezuma 2008). The notoriously unregulated buses proved to be dirty, inefficient, and their route expansions helped push disordered urban development at the city's margins, yet they were the most affordable means of getting around Bogotá for the vast majority of people. The unplanned explosion of automobile use in the 1960s and 1970s among the city's wealthy residents exacerbated the city's problems of disordered urban development. Sidewalks and parks, already few in number and neglected, became parking areas for cars. Ever-increasing numbers of buses, taxis, and cars competed for space on streets where minimal investment was made to maintain street infrastructure or even enforce traffic rules (Ardila and Menckhoff 2002). Throughout the 1980s and 1990s, chaotic driving, traffic jams, and pollution were a daily reality, and even though fewer than 15 percent of the people got around by private car, the situation had negative consequences for pretty much everybody. Partly in response to these crises, a new Colombian constitution passed in 1991 provided citizens with the "right to public space," but there were practically no places in Bogotá in which to exercise it.

A convergence of political factors interrupted these patterns and set the stage for a change in the status quo, including reforms begun in the late 1980s allowing for mayoral elections, greater city autonomy, and more effective tax collection, as well as the successive election of two charismatic and visionary mayors between 1994 and 2003 (Martin and Ceballos 2004; Montezuma 2005; Berney 2010). These mayors, Antanas Mockus (1994–1997, 2000–2003) and Enrique Peñalosa (1997–2000), brought distinct emphases to the office— Mockus developed social programs to combat violence and promote what he called a "culture of citizenship" which he argued was historically absent, while Peñalosa focused heavily on implementing "bricks and mortar" infrastructure projects—but their administrations shared a consistent commitment to using city resources and policies to ensure the right to the city and its public spaces for the social masses by simultaneously prioritizing security, social justice, and quality of life (Martin and Ceballos 2004; Beckett and Godoy 2010; Buendía 2010). As Mayor Peñalosa asserted, "In order for . . . cities [in the developing world] to prosper they must provide happiness for their citizens. This happiness doesn't come from individual wealth, but quality of life . . . it is our competitive edge" (quoted in Hagen 2003: 76).

Since more than 80 percent of the population did not own cars, but still had to bear the problems caused by them, taking on the negative social and environmental effects of automobile and bus use was an important manifestation of this commitment for both mayoral administrations (Montezuma 2006). To deal with persistent traffic jams and pedestrian inconvenience caused by drivers blocking intersections, the first Mockus administration famously replaced the traffic police for a period in 1995 with several hundred mime artists who used performance art to gently mock drivers and "show" them how to safely and properly pass through intersections (and it was actually effective; see Dalsgaard 2009 and Buendía 2010). It also began constructing pedestrian avenues, replacing sidewalks, expanding *Ciclovía*, and holding other events in public streets. It also drew up plans for an extensive bicycle network (Mockus was an everyday cyclist himself who once explained to reporters that he rode his bicycle to work

Figure 3.5 **No Car Day in Bogotá, February 24, 2000.**
Credit: AFP/Getty Images

to "maintain my sense of integrity and identity"; Dalsgaard 2009). Peñalosa's administration went further in curbing the automobile and constructing alternative mobility options. It raised gasoline taxes on automobiles and only allowed 40 percent of the city's cars to circulate at certain times; expanded the number of car-free activities (Figure 3.5), grew *Ciclovía* and the city bureaucracy to run it further; replaced the unregulated and inefficient private bus system with a city-controlled bus rapid transit system called *Transmilenio*; built desirable destinations in poor neighborhoods, such as public libraries and parks; renovated and expanded hundreds of public squares, parks, and sidewalks; and built the city's bicycle network, the *Cicloruta* (Ardila and Menckhoff 2002).

In spite of their broad popular support, the policies and changes to the city's physical form during the Mockus and Peñalosa years nevertheless provoked controversy. Wealthy political foes almost impeached Peñalosa, the transformation of the bus system was received with hostility by bus company owners, and plans for the bicycle network in particular drew sharp criticism. Critics expressed skepticism that anybody would use bicycle facilities, argued that attention to bicycles was a frivolous waste in such a needy city, or worried that trees and green space would be lost in the construction of bikeways. But Peñalosa pointed to studies the city commissioned indicating that conditions of population density and mixed land use were highly favorable for bicycle transportation, and more importantly that greater use of bicycles supported his broader social agenda, noting the "bike path is the only place where people can see them-selves as equals" (Ardila and Menckhoff 2002). As Peñalosa has been fond of saying, a person with a $30 bicycle has the same right to the city as a person with a $30,000 car, and he expressed the importance of raising what he called "bicycle consciousness" to ensure that the option of getting around by bicycle, especially for young and carless individuals, should have the same social legiti-macy and legal status as any other (Peñalosa 2002).

Importantly, the political initiatives described here were made in a top-down fashion by municipal administrators with minimal civic participation (Berney 2010). Nevertheless, in relation to the bicycle, civil society responded by creating a number of unique (for Bogotá at least) groups in support of the city's efforts to promote everyday bicycle use, such as *Bicibogotá* (Bikebogotá), *Mejor en Bici* (Better by Bike), and *La Vida en Bicicleta* (Life on a Bicycle). Prominent groups like the Bogotá Chamber of Commerce have also identified closely with the promotion of bicycle use (CCB 2009). Furthermore, although most trips in the city are made by public transit (75 percent) and private automobile (14 percent), these efforts did generate a measurable growth in the numbers of trips made by bicycles, from less than 1 percent to (depending on the source) between 2.3 percent and 4 percent of overall trips (Pardo 2010).

Ten years after these influential mayoral administrations, the pressures on the city's reinvented transportation system are high—the Transmilenio bus system has maxed out its capacity, the maintenance of the Cicloruta suffers, and the political momentum for building new infrastructure has stagnated (Pardo 2010). Further, the national traffic code treats bicycles and motorcycles the same, which has led to enforcement inconsistencies. Yet perceptions of the city have begun to shift, as have perceptions about bicycle riding in it. The reasons people give for riding are various—individuals refer to bicycling as a healthy way to get around, that it's non-polluting in a highly polluted city, and that it is convenient since it is quicker than getting around by bus or car (Dávila Valencia 2010: 185–186; Pardo 2010). As one rider expresses, "It's the most rapid, ecological, economical and fun option, even with problems of insecurity and few parking options" (quoted in Dávila 2010: 185). Economics factors especially heavily in Bogotaños' motivations to ride, with 60 percent of riders recently surveyed emphasizing that they ride bicycles because it is the least expensive form of getting around the city (IDU 2011). In fact, in terms of everyday bicycle use, Peñalosa's class-sensitive vision of "bicycle consciousness" in which the young and carless use bicycles to gain access to the city has borne fruit: the bulk of everyday riders using facilities like the *Cicloruta* are the poor, the unemployed, working-class laborers, and students (CCB 2009; IDU 2011; Brussel and Zuidgeest 2012).

Bicycle ownership is widespread in the city. About half of Bogotá's households have at least one bicycle, with Asian-produced mountain bikes being the most common bicycle type, since they are both rugged for city use and inexpensive. In spite of this high rate of household ownership, however, the actual riding of bicycles for everyday use is highly gendered. Young men constitute the majority of riders (86 percent), most of them between the ages of twenty and forty (CCB 2009). Because many of these individuals live distant from their places of work or study, average trip distances are of 8 to 9 kilometers—a factor that also limits the desire of many to ride (Wallace 2011). Enthusiasm for riding bicycles during Sunday and holiday *Ciclovías* is high—literally hundreds of thousands of bicycles can be seen on city streets, many of them ridden by women and children who normally won't ride during the week—yet numbers of cyclists using the *Cicloruta* on a daily basis still pale in comparison, carrying on average 170,000 people, mostly young men, per day (IDU 2011).

Conditions of bicycle infrastructure and cycling norms contribute to these disparities. During *Ciclovía*, for example, numbers of automobiles and their speed in the city are generally low, and city attendants direct traffic where cars and bicycles meet. In contrast, everyday use of the bicycle, even in the *Cicloruta*, engages regularly with automobiles. Although accident rates and cyclist fatalities have dropped by 70 percent and 62 percent respectively since the opening of the *Cicloruta* (CCB 2009), one rider observes, "To have to make way where there is no *cicloruta* is a high magnitude risk, it means flirting with taxis, bus drivers, drivers who don't know how to use their rearview mirrors, but know very well how to use their horns. To pass through a *cicloruta* also has its risk: crossroads where streets meet are like storms in which priority goes to the cars" (Dávila 2010: 191, see Figure 3.6). These rhythms vary throughout the day and are appreciated by cyclists in particular ways—as another cyclist observes, "If it's rush hour, the city seems totally chaotic, generating more and more visual contamination, sound, gases, but when it's not rush hour it feels very calm, relaxed, pretty" (quoted in Dávila 2010: 189). Other factors shaping bicycling experience include the lack of route connectivity in the Cicloruta, ubiquitous potholes, inadequate signage, unclear signals, and trash and other obstructions in the lanes (Pardo 2010; IDU 2011; Mike's Bogotá Bike Blog 2012).

The perception of insecurity and the city's reputation for robberies and other street crimes also shape cycling experience, one effect being an influence on route choice and heightened perceptions about which areas of the *Cicloruta* are safe (or not) to move on. As Dávila Valencia (2010: 192) observes: "some places of daily circulation are so dangerous that those who pass through them are obligated to make long detours that takes them a longer time than they had planned; these to avoid being grabbed. Some of the places are paths, solitary risky places where some of the population hide, sleep, which can lend itself to risky situations without a policeman or city official who ensures the passage of cyclists moving through." Perceptions of safety differ according to social position,

Figure 3.6 **Traffic and Pedestrians on Carrera 7, One of Bogotá's Busiest Thoroughfares.**
Credit: Paul Kennedy

such as class, age, and gender. Women cyclists, in particular, are considered especially vulnerable in this regard, although numbers of women using bicycles for everyday transportation have been growing, especially middle-class women (IDU 2011; Dávila 2012). *Ciclovía*, apparently, is also not immune from the perception of insecurity, with robberies of bicycles being reported as one of the most common street crimes during these events (Mike's Bogota Bike Blog 2011).

Bogotá's successes at building a bicycle system and bicycle-related events like *Ciclovía* have been attributed to leadership, political will, and effective city institutions (Ardila and Menckhoff 2002; Berney 2010). But even as these factors have had the power to reshape urban space and perceptions about the city, they still have not necessarily succeeded in producing a widespread commitment among Bogotaños to use bicycles to get around in their everyday lives. In addition to ongoing concerns about security, bicycles are still widely thought of as vehicles of the poor and marginalized, while automobiles are considered vehicles of the middle class and wealthy. What this means perhaps more than anything is in Bogotá there is still a gap between a political rhetoric of cultivating "bicycle consciousness" and what actual people think about getting around by bicycle.

BURLINGTON: Sharing the Road in a "Bicycle Friendly Community"

During the Fall of 2011, Burlington—Vermont's largest city, with 42,000 people—received word that its application to renew its status as a "Bicycle Friendly Community" was approved at the Silver level, one step above the Bronze rating it earned in 2005 (League of American Bicyclists 2012). The BFC program, which is run by the national advocacy group, the League of American Bicyclists, recognizes U.S. cities for their "bicycle friendliness" with ratings (from lowest to highest) of Bronze, Silver, Gold, or Platinum (see Box 3.2 for a closer look at this program). There are substantial practical differences between a top level city, such as the Platinum city of Portland, Oregon, and a city at the third level Silver like Burlington, not just in the quality and quantity of bicycle facilities and programs, but also the proportion of people who get around by bicycle on an everyday basis.[13]

Box 3.2 Defining Urban "Bicycle Friendliness": A Closer Look at the American "Bicycle Friendly Communities" Program

In contrast with the Netherlands, which has national bicycle policies that help influence the shape of bicycling in a city like Amsterdam, U.S. federal and state governments tend to have relatively little direct oversight over how and why a city might develop in ways that promote everyday bicycle use. These entities do provide funding and basic technical guidelines for road markings, signage, etc., but much is left to municipalities and their departments of public works to define and implement actual bicycle programs and infrastructure. For technical support and advice, cities often turn to private groups, such as the League of American Bicyclists and bicycle planning and engineering firms.

Since 1996, the League of American Bicyclists has run the "Bicycle Friendly Community" awards program to assess, recognize, encourage, and highlight the efforts of U.S. cities and suburbs that have cultivated conditions favorable for everyday bicycle use. As of 2012, 214 cities (including New York City, Chicago, San Francisco, and Minneapolis) have received an award, as have numerous smaller cities and suburbs. Receiving a BFC award does not carry any financial rewards, but it does provide a city with bragging rights, as well as a chance to undergo a systematic assessment of its bicycling conditions and to receive technical assistance. The application, which is a self-reporting questionnaire of over 80 detailed questions filled out by city officials and members of the community, is judged by a national panel of bicycle advocates and planners, as well as bicycling and transportation experts familiar with the applicant community.

A closer look at the application will give a better sense of what criteria are used currently by professional bicycle advocates in the American context to define urban "bicycle friendliness."

The application is organized into five sections referred to as "the Five Es," the goal being to provide a holistic picture of everyday cycling conditions:

Engineering: On-the-ground conditions for cyclists, including detailed information about how many bicycle lanes or paths are available; bicycle-specific signage or signals; road conditions and repairs, etc.

Education: Educational programs that exist to inform motorists and cyclists about sharing the road safely; maps or other information to aid cyclists; classes that teach safe cycling skills, etc.

Encouragement: Promotional efforts that exist to encourage cycling, such as Bike to Work activities; commuter incentive programs; bicycle parks and clubs, etc.

Enforcement: Relationship that exists between cyclists and the law enforcement community, including targeted enforcement of infractions against cyclists; the existence of special laws to protect cyclists; police who get around by bicycle, etc.

Evaluation and Planning: Efforts to plan for and evaluate ongoing programs and improvements in infrastructure; the existence of a bicycle master plan; data collection to inform improvements, etc.

In order to be considered for an award, the applicant must show accomplishment in each category. Not all applicants receive recognition, but all applicants receive a document from the League of American Bicyclists making recommendations about how to improve in each of these areas. An award lasts a four-year period.

Opportunities for Reflection and Action

Review the BFC program website (http://www.bikeleague.org/programs/bicyclefriendlyamerica/communities/), download the application, and read through it. Do you think the criteria found in the application are the only criteria that make a community "bicycle friendly"? What kinds of other issues might you introduce that shape (positively or negatively) the experience of cycling in a community? As a useful activity to better understand how this process works, consider filling out the application for your own community. Interview relevant city officials, bicycle and alternative transportation advocates, police, and others who might have knowledge of these conditions.

Nevertheless, Burlington's BFC ranking places it in elite company, among the top sixty American cities (out of the 214 recognized) for conditions that support everyday bicycle use. Other cities at the Silver level include several large cities that have made high-profile commitments to increasing urban bicycle transportation recently, including New York City and Chicago. Surprising, perhaps, for a small New England city that's snowy and somewhat hilly, but in fact many of the cities in the U.S. with the strongest commitments to cycling are not the Chicagos or New Yorks, but those with populations of less than 300,000 people. These have tended to have relatively greater success than bigger cities in creating higher volumes of cycling because of less automobile traffic, higher densities, shorter distances due to mixed land use development patterns, and limited options for public transit (Krizek 2012). Furthermore, cities with colleges and universities (of which Burlington has several) often have higher rates of cycling than other cities, given residential concentrations of young people who may not have access to automobiles.

Locally, word that Burlington won the Silver award registered with few residents, and except for a brief announcement in a mayor's office newsletter and a posting on the website of the city's main alternative transportation advocacy group, there was little attempt to publicize it. Bicycle advocates were generally pleased with the award, but some expressed informally surprise and ambivalence about the notion that the city had become "more bicycle friendly" since its last application. As one bicycle activist told me, "Silver? That's great. But really? We're resting on our laurels. So many other cities have been doing more than us to make it better for cyclists. Maybe on paper we look good, but on the streets it doesn't feel much better." Nevertheless, in its feedback to Burlington, the BFC program emphasized that the city exhibits numerous qualities that meet the program's expectations in the areas of the "Five Es," ranging from numerous bike lanes and other on-road facilities and an active bicycle advocacy scene to city policies intended to support bicycle transportation.[14] The document also notes that Burlington's bicycle "mode share" (the percentage of trips made by bicycle) is above the average for other U.S. cities (see Box 3.3 for a deeper consideration of this issue).

In spite of these conditions, Burlington's bicycle network is regarded locally, by cyclists and advocates at least, as piecemeal and underdeveloped. The network consists of painted lines on a small and inconsistent number of the city's streets, signage is often inconspicuous, and there are weak and unreliable bicycle parking options even though a parking ordinance requires most commercial establishments to provide at least a few spots. Further, there are no consistent north–south routes with bicycle facilities and only a few east–west routes (the two major axes of travel in the city), bicycle lanes end with little apparent logic, recommended bicycle routes are often heavy with automobile

Box 3.3 The Production of Traffic Data and the Invisibility of Cyclists

There is (perhaps) a surprising amount to be said regarding claims about Burlington's bicycle mode share, the main thing being that nobody is really sure exactly what it is. Like many cities in the U.S., there is no systematic data collection in Burlington about everyday bicycle travel or the demographics of cyclists, although some data has been collected about users of the city's lakeside bicycle path. Instead Burlingtonians have relied on national surveys to provide information—such as the Federal Highway Administration's "National Household Travel Survey," or the Census Bureau's "American Community Survey," surveys that sample a small percentage of the population in which respondents self-report how they get to and from work—as well as on state and county traffic counts that include pedestrians but not cyclists (Smart Mobility Inc. 2010; Litman 2012). Travel surveys often overlook or undercount the kinds of trips that are more likely to be made by non-motorized means, such as shorter trips, non-work trips, off-peak trips, non-motorized links of motorized trips, children's travel, and recreational travel (Litman 2011). They also often tend to combine bicyclists and walkers into the same "bike/ped" category.

The result is that different surveys yield different data, and cyclists are often invisible in the data that gets produced. According to the Census Bureau's ACS, for example, which combines walking and bicycle trips, non-motorized trips to work in Burlington are just above 23 percent (the national rate is 3.4 percent), but it doesn't separate out bicycling. The NHTS pegs bicycling to work at 1.3 percent of trips, but it too focuses solely on trips to work. The lack of data and uncertainties produced about overall rates of bicycle travel do have consequences: although practical bicycle use is probably more common than these percentages suggest, political decisions about transportation infrastructure and program priorities are influenced by estimations of travel demand that rely, in part, on these kinds of data. If bicycles are hardly visible in the data, then it is harder to make the case of their relevance in urban transportation planning decisions.

There are many reasons why there is little or no collection of urban cycling data, including lack of dedicated funding for it; the perception that there is not enough bicycle or pedestrian activity to justify the expense; the challenges of getting accurate counts; and a broad cultural framing of cycling as leisure and recreation, not as transportation.

traffic, and arterials in and out of the city are high-speed roads with few or no accommodations for bicycles.

The city council has in the past decade passed various land use and transportation plans that envision the development of a "multi-modal" transportation system in which increasing bicycle transportation, along with increasing opportunities for walking and public transit, are viewed as playing a key role.[15] Visions of a city full of protected bike lanes fill these documents. The broader goal driving these plans is to reduce automobile use and emissions to protect the historic character of the city's streetscape, to improve the quality of life in the city's neighborhoods, and to help the city achieve climate change-related carbon reduction goals—the last of which was a prominent initiative of a recent mayor. Yet much of the vision laid out in these documents has gone unrealized due to a deep history of prioritizing transportation investments to benefit motorized transit over non-motorized, a limited bicycle program with a small annual budget, economic recession and other city financial troubles, as well as a committee-driven city political structure that has led to slow and incomplete adoption of transportation and land use plans (see also Ober 2010).

As a result, what Burlington's current version of 'multi-modalism' entails from the point of view of the bicycle can best be described as "share the road." Placing limits on automobiles is a highly unpopular issue among city merchants and commuters, so sharing the road is more than a catchy bumper sticker slogan: it is a politically and economically expedient orientation to integrating bicycles into city traffic. It is rooted in the idea that in the absence of a protected and separate network for bicyclists, bicycle riders must accommodate themselves to the rules and rhythms of the motor vehicle system.

The notion of sharing the road is an old one, predating the automobile's arrival in Burlington, although what it means in practice and in legal terms has shifted over time. Bicycles made their appearance in Burlington during the 1880s, when its proximity to New England bicycle factories, its population of well-to-do merchants and industrialists, and the growing popularity of bicycle touring in the countryside fueled the rise of "wheeling" as a leisure activity. The city saw the creation of several "wheelmen's clubs," and the city's macadamized streets (a type of smooth pavement made of finely crushed rock) were considered ideal for bicycle riding. In the 1890s, the city experienced the cycling craze that swept throughout much of the U.S. and women also took to bicycles (Figure 3.7). There were ten bicycle dealers in this city of 10,000 people, more than twice the number there are today with more than four times the population. Bicycle races and parades were common spectacles in the city and Burlingtonians played a prominent role in the state and national-level movements to promote good roads. Yet the bicycle's rapid rise provoked social controversies, and to deal with growing conflicts cyclists were having with

Figure 3.7 **Burlington "New Women" Take to the Bicycle.**
Source: Courtesy of Glenn Eames.

walkers, horses, and carriage drivers, the city passed an 1897 bicycle ordinance aimed at regulating the sharing of the road by setting a bicycle speed limit in the city center and requiring lights at night.

With the turn of the century, an oversupply of bicycles coincided with the coming of the automobile, which led elites toward automobiles and to the shuttering of all but two bicycle sellers. A new "Gentlemen's Driving Club" was established, a car dealer opened, and in 1903 Burlington resident Horatio Nelson Jackson gained national fame by becoming the first person to drive a motor car across the U.S. In the coming decades, cars were too expensive except for the city's wealthiest, and the city's electric street car system, bicycles, and extensive sidewalks met many peoples' daily mobility needs. During the first half of the twentieth century, bicycles began to be more associated with children and cyclists were increasingly displaced by automobiles in the city's streets.

After the Second World War, regional development patterns became increasingly (and continue to be) organized around low-density suburbanization, and arterial roads were retrofitted to carry growing numbers of automobiles to and from residential subdivisions and strip mall commercial centers. A new interstate highway was built, which helped fuel the development of outlying suburbs. In the 1960s, an outer ring expressway surrounding Burlington was begun but never completed, stymied by neighborhood activists and an increasingly assertive local environmental movement (Troy 2012). With increasing motorization and sprawl, bicycles had become practically unknown as a means of everyday mobility in the region during the middle years of the twentieth century.

Nevertheless, new meanings about bicycles began circulating during this period, as a sporting good (with the founding of the Green Mountain Bicycle Club, a racing and sport-oriented group, in 1968), and as a means to overcome the challenges of the oil crisis of the early 1970s. Unlike the first bicycle boom, in which bicycles were prized as progressive machines, interest in bicycles during this period was mostly viewed as an alternative to the automobile. The idea that the bicycle was a "vehicle" was formalized in new state legislation, including a 1973 law defining bicycles as vehicles with the same rights and responsibilities as motor vehicles—the formalization of a contemporary "share the road" practice. In Burlington, new efforts were also made to promote bicycling, primarily as a response to problems associated with the automobile. According to a 1974 city Alderman's report, there were an estimated 13,000 cyclists in the city (about a third of the city's population) and 75 percent of new bikes were sold to adults. It expressed that conditions were favorable for a new bicycle ordinance and that building a new bikeway system would help reduce traffic congestion, improve health, and provide recreational opportunities.

The bikeway system envisioned in the early 1970s was never built, but in subsequent years various social and political pressures generated new opportunities for the bicycle's rise in the city. One was an environmentalist campaign in the late 1970s to convert the city's old waterfront to a greenway (a multi-use path of scenic beauty) and public park, an effort that eventually led to the creation of a seven and a half-mile recreational bike path along the city's lakefront. Pressure on the city to maintain economic competitiveness in the face of ongoing suburbanization led city leaders to back the idea of other car-free recreational public spaces, including the conversion of the city's main commercial street into a pedestrian mall. Although the primary value of these projects lay in enhancing the city's tourism and recreational potential, they injected new life into discussions about bicycles, and in 1990—earlier than many American cities—the city formed a bicycle advisory council to assist the Department of Public Works in identifying opportunities to improve conditions for bicycles on the streets, a move that laid the groundwork for the rise of a more formal bicycle advocacy community in the city (see Chapter 4). During the 1990s and 2000s, greater use of bicycles has been viewed as consistent with a self-image Burlington has developed as a politically progressive small city with a unique social fabric that prioritizes quality of life, historic preservation, a healthy population, and environmental sustainability.

These perceptions of the city are often reflected in the ways cyclists talk about why they ride today. As one woman in her thirties explained to me:

> I do it because it feels good, it connects me to my community, it is clean, it is simple. When I get to where I'm going, I feel refreshed. It clears my head. It's convenient too. I usually get places I need to go faster than when I'm in a car. And I think Burlington is a better place when there is one less car taking up space and polluting the air. Yeah, bicycling just seems like a Burlington thing. It's green, healthy, neighborly, not like that metal box that cuts you off from the community around you.

For many individuals, often those with cars (including this one), riding a bicycle is perceived as a choice and as an exercise of individual agency and autonomy from the automobile. It can even be a political expression, sometimes coupled with a "one less car" sticker on a frame or a fender. But this notion of choice is not the case for all riders, among them college students—who often express that they ride bicycles because they "have no choice" (the assumption being that driving a car, which they don't have access to, would be a better choice)—and low-income residents, many of whom are recent refugees from Africa and Southeast Asia who have access to recycled bicycles through an initiative to provide bicycles to low income residents. As one Congolese refugee who uses his bike, the public bus, or catches a ride from a friend to get to and from his job as a janitor observed to me, "I like my bike. It gets me to work some days. But I would rather have a car."

Although no reliable demographic indicators profiling Burlington cyclists exist, there is a perception locally that the profile of everyday riders in Burlington is socially heterogeneous and differentiated. As one long-time resident and former bike shop owner described it when I asked him to describe everyday bicycle users: "It's quite a mixed scene! You have the homeless and bottle collectors—they use their bikes in ways I think all bikes should be used, as a primary vehicle. Then there are the new refugees which for many of them a bike is all they can afford. There are the college kids, since a lot of them don't have cars. In smaller numbers you have the bike commuters who live out in the suburbs, and then people who live downtown who like me believe it's easy and quick and clean to get around by bicycle. Thing is, we're not all alike by any stretch. It's like a bunch of different tribes on bikes." One expression of that diversity is reflected in the bicycles one sees around the city, which range from high-end road bikes or mountain bikes to "beaters," old, somewhat battered bicycles that might be mountain bikes, road bikes, three speeds, or other bicycle types. A minority of these bicycles will be deliberately set up as practical vehicles with racks, baskets, or bags for carrying things.

That heterogeneity and differentiation is reflected as well in the practices and skills exhibited by different cyclists, and the abilities cyclists believe are necessary to get around on bicycle. First, it is necessary to observe that bicycle mobility is highly seasonal, with only a relative handful of cyclists continuing to get around by bicycle during the winter, which is not only cold and snowy but hard on bicycles because the anti-icing materials the city puts on sidewalks and streets generate corrosion and rust on bicycles. Unlike some northern cities where snow is common, including Amsterdam, Burlington does not plow streets with bicycles in mind. Whatever the case, when I've asked interviewees to characterize the issues they face in getting around the city by bicycle, a common response focuses on the uncertainties involved in the activity. Those uncertainties range from the conditions of the street network—bike lanes and shoulders commonly have ruts, grates, sand, or other obstacles, and bike lanes sometimes simply end with no directions for the cyclist—to the actions of pedestrians and other cyclists—one concern being whether or not other cyclists are following traffic rules, which are inconsistent at best.

More important are the actions of motorists, never far from the thoughts of bicycle riders in Burlington, which express themselves in a heightened awareness about traffic conditions and the actions and attitudes of motorists. As one man expressed to me, this awareness is different from what he feels when he is driving a car: "I'm usually zoned when I'm driving my car, focused on the car in front of me. But riding on a bike I have a different awareness, of everything that is going on around me. You know, I'm just so aware of what cars are doing all around me. Maybe that one coming up behind me will hit me from behind, that one coming toward me will pull in front of me, or someone in a parked car will open the door on me." Although a number of signs on the city's roads inform cyclists of their right to the road ("Cyclists May Take Full Lane" signs have been showing up in recent years), motorists do not themselves take it for granted—remember Zach's story at the beginning of this chapter—and bicycle riders have differing abilities and confidence about sharing the road with automobiles whose speeds average 25 to 30 mph, which is beyond the capability of even the most athletic and seasoned riders to keep up with. Furthermore, there is a common perception among drivers and even cyclists themselves that the space of urban streets is not for non-motorized transportation (Figure 3.8).

One major strategy for dealing with the uncertainties produced by riding among cars is to develop skills that involve practices like the use of hand signals and positioning oneself in the street safely to allow cars to pass or to communicate where one is headed, as well as a sense of confidence and trust that if one is predictable and visible, drivers will accommodate a cyclist. Although bicycle

Figure 3.8 **"Bicycles Take Full Lane" Sign on a Busy Road.**
Source: Author's Own.

advocacy groups teach these skills in Burlington, most cyclists I've interviewed who practice them report that they never formally learned how to ride with automobile traffic. As Zach, whose brief story opens this chapter, explained: "I simply observed others, I try to act as a car might, [and] get out of the way when things get hairy, but stand my ground when I need the space on the road."

A more common approach for dealing with those uncertainties is strategic avoidance. Route choice plays a role in this. As one man in his forties who rides three miles each way to work everyday expressed: "I go out of my way to avoid roads with a lot of cars on them. My route to work has me going up a big hill and it actually takes longer than if I was on the main street cars are on. But I don't want the stress." Another strategy is sidewalk riding, which is ubiquitous throughout the city except in the city center where it is prohibited. Young kids getting to and from school in particular are highly likely to ride on sidewalks, although beyond this group membership in a particular social category such as gender, ethnicity, or class does not map easily onto sidewalk riding. Sidewalk riding, which can create conflicts with pedestrians and carries dangers of its own as motorists pull in and out of driveways, is viewed variously as a matter of individual choice and necessary for one's safety (as one woman observed, "I don't ride much in traffic. I don't have much confidence in my abilities and I don't trust drivers. I feel like having the sidewalk gives me a choice to feel safer") or as a matter of mutual convenience (according to one young man, "I stay out their way and they stay out of mine."). Sidewalk riding is also highly contextual; many riders slip onto streets when automobile traffic is minimal or pedestrians are in the way.

Perceptions of vulnerability and risk are variable, and closely tied to individual perception as well as social position. One common stereotype is that women, in particular, are risk averse—which implies not liable ride a bicycle to begin with, more likely to ride on sidewalks, follow traffic rules, ride slowly, etc.—while young men embrace risk and disregard traffic rules. This argument is often used to explain why the current bicycle renaissance is gendered, with men making up most of the ridership (Pucher and Buehler 2011). As one woman who is a mother of several young children expressed to me, "You don't see women running through the stop signs like those young college guys! They're like demons, bombing down the hills." Notwithstanding the fact that careful observation shows young women doing these things, and young men riding cautiously on sidewalks, such perspectives are meaningful in that they are part of a broader gendered discourse about who is more apt to ride and in what ways one should ride. The reality is that decisions to ride bicycles, as well as how they are ridden, depend not just how someone sees themselves in relation to the activity of cycling and sharing the road with automobiles, but a combination of practical factors like the distance one needs to go, the purpose of the trip, the time of day, whether or not something needs to be carried, how many stops might be made, the desire for physical activity, and who else might be accompanying the rider (see also Krizek 2012).

The broader issue here is that differentiation, variability, and uncertainty are not simply qualities of the street network and other users, but they are of cyclists as well. That is, there is variability and differentiation in how cyclists behave as a social group: some ride on the streets and follow the rules of the road while others avoid the street when they can; some ride expensive and impractical racing bikes to get around while others ride modest bicycles especially set up for practical purposes; some ride because it's economically important to them or a temporary interruption in a car-centered life while others view it as a conscious expression of their lifestyle and political values. Perhaps what is held in common among these riders is not necessarily an agreed-upon common sense notion of what it means to be a bicycle rider—although periodically one sees evidence of that shared status as riders at a stoplight or stop sign acknowledge each other's existence with a nod or a hello, suggesting some kind of common recognition—but a sense that riding a bicycle through Burlington is an individualized performance shaped by the contours of one's own subjective perspectives, senses of risk and vulnerability, and personal strategies for sharing the road.

Conclusion

To say that bicycle riding is an individualized performance is only part of the equation here, however. Bicycling is also a collective, expressive, and culturally patterned experience, in the sense that it is organized and constrained by social and political-economic processes, symbolic meanings, and actual skills, practices, and norms involved in riding a bicycle though a city, each of which transcends what any single individual does or believes. From this vantage point, it is possible to see that processes of urban bicycle use are *constructed*, that is, actively created not just by momentous decisions of political and economic actors and institutions that impact the shape and structure of an urban mobility system, but also the rather mundane day-to-day decisions and shared meanings of those involved in actually moving around the streets. These activities and meanings are set against a backdrop in which the demand for mobility, as well as the reconfiguration of urban spaces that both accommodate and shape that demand, are closely tied to particular patterns of urban history and built environments that have far-reaching impacts on people's social relations and patterns of daily life.

There is no doubt that the construction of facilities, infrastructure, and policies specifically designed for bicycle riders have important impacts on the experience and motivation to ride a bicycle through a city. Riding on Amsterdam's and Bogotá's cycle tracks, for example, in which the experience of getting around the city requires minimal involvement with automobiles and provides direct, speedy, and predictable routes, is a lot different than sharing the road or going out of one's way to avoid riding with automobile traffic in Burlington. And the presence of cycle tracks entails the development of certain skills and norms, and it can even change people's perceptions of their urban environment, rendering them open to it in new and specific ways.

But it would be mistaken to think that cycle tracks alone, or other changes in the built environment—or for that matter, pro-bike policies and programs— can alone cause the magical transformation of a city into a bicycle-friendly place. Such "build-it-and-they-will-come" thinking is a form of technological determinism, a belief that technical fixes drive social change. The case of Bogotá demonstrates the limitations of this thinking: even as city leaders have invested in what is considered widely to be a world-class bicycle network, cultural attitudes, social relations, and urban histories have conditioned and shaped people's attitudes toward not just the bicycle but toward the urban spaces in which the use of a bicycle takes place. The fact that these perceptions and attitudes are so powerful helps explain why daily cycling is still limited—the thinking being that only poor people ride bicycles for transportation, or the perception that areas of the city's *Cicloruta* remain chaotic and dangerous. At the same time, it may also explain why *Ciclovías* are widely popular since they involve the bicycle in recreational and leisure-oriented ways.

The other dimension here is that technological determinism views the promotion of urban bicycle use as a mostly apolitical activity, except perhaps when it involves the creation and enforcement of formal state policy. But even as state policy plays a role in shaping the conditions under which bicycle cultures are expressed, at the local level there are other forces pushing for change, which are the advocacy and social movements promoting everyday bicycle use. The next chapter explores how bicycle advocacy groups and activities deliberately politicize the bicycle in Burlington.

For Further Exploration

In recent years the flowering of interest in cities and bicycles has generated vigorous international discussions and many resources about how best to promote and understand the relationship between bicycling and cities. The Dutch, not surprisingly, have been at the forefront of these discussions and are proactive in sharing their experiences, through the Dutch Cycling Embassy (http://www.dutchcycling.nl/). The film "Cycling Friendly Cities" is a Dutch government production that highlights conditions that promote cycling: http://www.youtube.com/watch?v=5rwwxrWHBB8. Further north in Denmark, the popular cycling blog Copenhagenize (www.copenhagenize.com) is well-known not just for its discussions about cycling in Copenhagen but for its engagement with broader international discussions about cycling in cities.

The Canadian organization 8–80 Cities (based on the idea "If you create a city that's good for an eight-year-old and good for an 80-year-old, you will create a successful city for everyone.") promotes strategies for developing liveable streets and healthy communities around active transportation. 8–80 Cities: http://www.8-80cities.org/.

For a social scientific perspective on the relationship between cities, society, and cycling, a British sociology research project focusing on four cities that have relatively high rates of cycling has an interesting blog: http://cyclingcultures.org.uk/

For perspectives on actual cycling conditions in Amsterdam, see the film "How the Dutch Got Their Cycle Paths": http://bicycledutch.wordpress.com/2011/10/20/how-the-dutch-got-their-cycling-infrastructure/; visit the Fietsberaad (Dutch Cycling Council): http://www.fietsberaad.nl/index.cfm?lang=en; YouTube Channel based on user-generated content called "Cycling in the Netherlands": http://www.youtube.com/user/markenlei; and "Amsterdam Houdt Van Fietsen!" "Amsterdam Loves Bikes!": http://www.youtube.com/watch?v=EOkqTDdtlc4&feature=player_embedded#!

Several blogs report (in English) on the daily practice of bicycle mobility in Amsterdam and other cities in the Netherlands, including Bicycle Dutch (http://bicycledutch.wordpress.com/) and Amsterdamize (www.amsterdamize.com), both of which are operated by Dutch cyclists and media makers; Bakfiets en Meer (http://www.workcycles.com/blog) which is run by Workscycles, a bicycle manufacturer and shop; and A View from the Cycle Path (www.aviewfromthecyclepath.com), which although it is not focused on Amsterdam, has strong opinions and perspectives on cycling there. For a good description of a Dutch bicycle, see David Henbrow's entry "Anatomy of a reliable, everyday bicycle": http://www.aviewfromthecyclepath.com/2009/01/anatomy-of-reliable-everyday-bicycle.html

In the U.S., the Streetsblog website (www.streetsblog.net) and Streetfilm website (www.streetfilms.org) cover the latest news in major U.S. cities related to conditions, policies, and conflicts related to bicycling and other non-motorized transportation. The National Association of City Transportation Officials recently published an "Urban Bikeway Design" website as a major resource for bicycle planning. It provides city officials desiring to implement bicycle infrastructure with concrete technical advice and examples. See it here: http://nacto.org/cities-for-cycling/design-guide/.

Burlington bicycle cultures have not been closely studied, nor do discussions about it circulate widely online. Nevertheless, there is one short film called "Life Cycles" that examines Burlington's bicycle culture from one point of view: http://vimeo.com/11587451.

In 2007 and 2008, Streetfilms issued three short films about bicycling and public space in Bogotá: "Lessons from Bogotá" http://www.streetfilms.org/lessons-from-bogota/; "Riding Bogota's Bountiful Protected Bikeways" http://www.streetfilms.org/riding-bogotas-bountiful-protected-bikeways/; and "Ciclovía": http://www.streetfilms.org/ciclovia/. For an alternative and self-critical look at bicycle mobility issues in Bogotá, see Mike's Bogota Bike Blog (http://

mikesbogotabikeblog.blogspot.com/), and in particular this posting, which examines gaps and problems in the *Cicloruta*: http://mikesbogotabikeblog. blogspot.com/2012/08/the-return-of-26th-street-ciclovia.html

The Danish Film "Cities on Speed: Bogotá Change" is a lively and engaging documentary film that explores the changes made during the Mockus and Peñalosa administrations. It is available on YouTube here: http://www.youtube. com/watch?v=gyBe5-irc_4

4

"GOOD FOR THE CAUSE": THE BIKE MOVEMENT AS SOCIAL ACTION AND CULTURAL POLITICS

"The contest for us is not just policies and striping on the roads, it is, at a fundamental level, over meanings."

—Bicycle advocate in Burlington, Vermont, 2011

Bicycle advocacy has many expressions in Burlington, Vermont. One of the more recognizable ones is the "Critical Mass" ride. Begun in 1992 in San Francisco and now taking place on the last Friday of the month in over 300 cities worldwide, Critical Mass is a group ride in which cyclists pedal slowly during rush hour, not with a specific route in mind but to show a mass presence of bicycles on the streets. Envisioned as an expression of civil disobedience and advocacy for public spaces not dominated by automobiles, Critical Mass rides deliberately disrupt automobile traffic as they meander through a city: riders take a whole lane of traffic, stretch out over several blocks, run stop signs and red lights, and even occupy intersections briefly where they might stage a "die-in" or perform some other symbolic act to draw attention to the plight or rights of cyclists (Figure 4.1). The rides are cast as celebrations, not protests, and their organization is informal and decentralized in order to avoid the requirement of a police permit or potential reprisals against leaders. Nevertheless, in a few high-profile cases, such as in New York City, police have cracked down violently on Critical Mass rides, arguing that they disrupt the rights of others (Carlsson 2002).

Critical Mass in Burlington has never provoked a strong response from police, since city officials long ago grew accustomed to mass bike rides—several of these emphasizing nudity (including the global advocacy ride, the World Naked Bike Ride, and naked bike rides held at the end of every semester at the University of Vermont), and others expressive in different ways, such as a city-wide Halloween ride in October. Burlington's Critical Mass is typically quite small, rarely attracting more than a couple of dozen riders, and it doesn't happen every month but somewhat irregularly. Riders tend to ignore traffic signals and stop signs, but the emphasis is definitely less on confrontation and more on celebration. The ride can take on the appearance of a quixotic parade:

Figure 4.1 **Critical Mass, Hungary 2009.**
Credit: © 2010 AFP

costumed cyclists ride decorated bicycles, blow whistles and horns, and chant slogans like "We aren't blocking traffic. We *are* traffic!" or "Get out of your car. Get on your bike!" Given the celebratory tone, Critical Mass attracts a lot of young adults looking for a fun experience and who are somewhat apolitical about their participation, although some riders definitely view their participation as a political activity. As one semi-regular participant told me, "I do it because it's good for the cause, the bike cause."

Another expression of bicycle advocacy—which is also viewed as "good for the cause"—is the performance of "Intersection Actions," an activity that combines citizen interaction with intensive law enforcement at intersections with traffic signals. In an Intersection Action, volunteers gather for a couple of hours during the middle of the day at a busy intersection where accident rates are high, or where the potential for conflict between walkers, bicycle riders, and motorists is great because of a high volume of traffic (Figure 4.2). The volunteers, who don fluorescent vests, spread out and stand at each corner with some handouts, including coupons for local shops and traffic safety brochures, their goal being to interact with people on foot or on bicycle who show up at the corner. The volunteers stop those who "do good"—that is, who wait their turn to cross, don't walk or ride against the light, stay within the lines of the

Figure 4.2 **Intersection Action, 2010.**
Source: Author's Own.

cross-walk, etc.—and issue a ticket that looks a lot like a police citation except it is a "citation for good behavior," and then give away a coupon or two. To those who aren't following traffic rules, the volunteers attempt to explain what the rules are and why they should be followed. Meanwhile, the police officer is parked nearby in a cruiser, waiting to write up actual citations for motorists who run the signal or break the speed limit.

The Intersection Action is an initiative of a campaign called the "Safe Streets Collaborative," a joint effort of the city's police department, bicycle and pedestrian advocates, universities, and health institutions "to reduce crashes and injuries for people on foot and on bike by building a culture of respect on our streets and sidewalks." Coordinated by a local advocacy group, Local Motion, the Safe Streets Collaborative was formed several years ago in response to two incidents a week apart in which cyclists were severely injured at intersections, one by a hit-and-run motorist. The slogan of the campaign— "Give Respect, Get Respect. Safety is a Two Way Street."—is based on a philosophy that cyclists, pedestrians, and motorists all play a role in making roadways safer for people on foot and on bike. As one of its organizers explained to me, "It reframes bicycle and pedestrian issues away from a blame game or a conflict between cyclists and cars, and reminds everybody that the streets are a give-and-take relationship."

As efforts to change the culture of the streets, Critical Mass rides and Intersection Actions are both relatively new fronts in urban politics, and they clearly exhibit certain similarities. Both are intentionally disruptive and seek to change the symbolic meaning of city streets—from dangerous and hostile to safe and inviting—by addressing the one-sidedness of automobile domination and drawing attention to the alternative possibilities represented by non-motorized mobility. They also emphasize the protagonistic role cyclists can play in changing these meanings. And they each represent themselves as useful tools in a broader cause of improving conditions for people who ride bikes in the city. These days this cause is often referred to in Burlington and elsewhere as part of a broader "bike movement," a social movement based on the idea that collective action is necessary to pressure government and society to accept the everyday use of bicycles (Wray 2008; Mapes 2009).

Yet there are important differences here as well. Some of these differences are tactical: Intersection Actions are coordinated by an organization whose goal is to generate face-to-face interactions between individual citizens, while Critical Mass is functionally decentralized and the unplanned dynamics of the group moving as a mass through city streets define the experience. And Critical Mass plays up the spectacle of bicycle riding itself, while Intersection Actions focus on the mundane and everyday dimensions of bicycling *and* walking. Underlying these tactical differences is a deeper difference in political philosophy that has to do with conflicting orientations toward the rules, norms, and institutions that govern the urban traffic system, as well as the nature of citizen advocacy. Intersection Actions imagine law-abiding citizens upholding and reinforcing the system of rules and norms by educating other citizens about them, with the close support of law enforcement agencies. Critical Mass, with its intentions of civil disobedience, imagines citizens as resisting those rules and norms, exposing them as ineffective given the actual conditions of city streets. It seeks to present an alternative vision of how things should be, a condition in which empowered cyclists circulate through the city freely without intimidation by motorists. These differences can cause frustration and tension, especially among those critical of the outlaw tendencies and defiant attitude of Critical Mass rides, who are equally convinced that *rule-following* will generate free circulation of empowered cyclists without intimidation by motorists.

The customary view of social movements is that they are a form of social action in which an interest group with a progressive agenda engages in a struggle to transform power relations from the bottom up (Nash 2004), which in this case might mean something like marginalized cyclists standing up to assert their place on the streets. But these quick examples suggest two important things: first, social movements operate as much in the terrain of cultural meanings, ideas, moralities, symbols, and identities as they do in the arena of power relations; second, no social movement is monolithic. In the "bike movement" differing visions over what is "good for the cause"—the symbolic meanings and practical social actions necessary to achieve these things, as well as the desired outcomes these actions might produce—can generate divergent views about critical issues, such as what it means to collaborate with powerful institutions, the role of individual citizens in political processes, or the status of bicycles in creating changes in urban mobility patterns. The vision of the bike movement that emerges from such considerations is one of an unfolding, flexible, and emergent social and institutional arena. This arena has heterogeneous fronts where competing and sometimes contradictory ideas about how to make change on streets unfold through (sometimes uneasy) collaborations and the mobilization of people around particular symbolic claims or identities. In the midst of these dynamics, the meanings of basic categories—the bicycle, the street—are themselves diverse, unsettled, and contested, and the distinctiveness of the "bicycle cause" can blur with other causes.

This chapter offers ethnographic perspectives on the construction of bicycling as an urban social movement—as an idea around which people organize *and* as a diverse set of practices that aim to create urban change—both of which involve dynamics of "cultural politics," a concept that refers to the inextricable interrelationship between the cultural and political that takes place through the intersection of ideas, symbols, strategies, and social action in the contexts of social movements (Fox and Starn 1997; Alvarez et al. 1998). With the exception of the first section—which starts with a fieldwork story and then offers a brief historical overview of bicycle advocacy in the U.S. at the national level—this chapter is based on participant-observation and interviews among bicycle advocates in Burlington. The discussion here is organized around a basic but central issue: What are the meanings of the bicycle and bicycling among those participating in the bike movement? Rather than provide an exhaustive catalogue of all the possible answers to this question, which would require description of all the many contexts in which bicycle advocacy takes place in Burlington, the discussion focuses on several strategically chosen case studies that illustrate the heterogeneous and contextual ways urban bicycle advocates imagine and act to promote the bicycle in everyday contexts.

Constructing a Bike Movement with a Politically Flexible Symbol

"You are the heroes of the cycling movement in this country! Make no mistake: it's a movement." Thus began an address by Representative Earl Blumenauer, a powerful Oregon congressman associated closely with the promotion of bicycles in federal transportation policy, to the 800 attendees of the 2012 National Bike Summit in Washington, D.C. The Summit, which is organized by the League of American Bicyclists and the bicycle industry's lobbying arm Bikes Belong, is billed as the nation's largest and most important gathering of bicycle advocates. It takes place every March and draws an eclectic assortment of professional bicycle advocates, charity ride and race organizers, bicycle club members, bicycle manufacturers, retailers and shop owners, urban planners, and officials from city, state, and federal government, each of whom engages with bicycles in distinctive (although sometimes overlapping) ways—as business, policy, sport, recreation, or transportation. What unifies them at the Summit is, perhaps, a shared commitment to developing and articulating a politics to increase the everyday use of bicycles across the U.S. Participants—most of whom are white, male, over the age of 40, and middle-class—come to the Summit to network, share information about their failures, successes, and dilemmas in advocacy, and get fired up to "storm Capitol Hill," that is, make visits to Congressional offices to articulate the case for why the federal government should continue to formally support bicycle infrastructure and programs, which it has been doing since 1991. The relationship between bicycles and transportation policy is thus a big issue here: the Summit has numerous workshops to introduce participants to the details of federal transportation bills and train them in the protocols of citizen advocacy in the U.S. Congress. The whole thing also has a strong peprally feel, and it was Blumenauer's job to pump up the attendees for their visits to Capitol Hill.

In his speech Blumenauer described how, despite the palpable momentum the national cycling movement had gained in generating public interest and investment in cycling during the past few years, the current political environment on Capitol Hill was growing hostile to a key pillar of the bicycle movement's agenda—maintaining federal funding for bicycle programs—due to the influence of a strongly partisan element in the House of Representatives ("Tea Party" Republicans) that wants to reduce federal spending. Add to this a Congressional culture of mistrust and antagonism resulting from deep partisan divides—and the fact that bicycle transportation is often implicitly identified as a "liberal" issue—and the situation was fragile for bicycles. But he emphasized that the bicycle transcends political partisanship, opening the door to a new kind of partisanship. As he said, "We can use a cycling metaphor. *Bike partisanship* is a way to bring people together again."

This notion of "bike partisanship" as a means to transcend, or maybe better, to navigate political and ideological differences reemerged on multiple occasions over the course of the Summit, as other visiting politicians and their staffers, as well as bicycle industry lobbyists and advocates, shared strategies with participants about how to tailor the pro-bicycle message to the political environment. Special emphasis was placed on framing the bicycle as a matter of economic growth and job creation (to make jobs for transportation workers, the bicycle industry, and small businesses); federal austerity (because bike infrastructure is less expensive to build and maintain than automobile infrastructure, and federal health care costs will be reduced with a healthier population); national security (to reduce dependence on foreign oil); and as a symbol of American personal independence and self-reliance (because bicycles are self-powered). What is important about these claims is not that they were framing bicycles in a politically-neutral fashion, but that they were attempting to come up with specific symbolic meanings to appeal to a particular set of (though nobody said it, "conservative") political values currently dominating in Congress.

This kind of sensitivity to the flexibility of the bicycle as a political symbol has a long history, going back to the late nineteenth century when a diverse array of political, economic, and social interests strategically appropriated the bicycle to advance their causes. Among these groups were feminists, for whom the bicycle symbolized women's emancipation from constricting social norms and fueled the right to vote, and socialists, who viewed the bicycle as a useful tool to spread political literature on routes between Boston and New York City (Furness 2010: 38).[1] Col. Albert Pope also understood that symbolic flexibility when he founded the country's first and (still) most prominent national bicycle advocacy group, the League of American Wheelmen (now the League of American Bicyclists). He successfully framed it as an effort to generate political reform for the rights of a progressive new force in American society—the bicycle and its emerging industries—and to advance the cause of creating better roads for more efficient travel, trade, and national development, (mostly) avoiding the possibility that such advocacy would instead be viewed as a selfish endeavor to advance his own interests. As the 1890s bicycle boom faded and bicycles produced in the U.S. became more oriented toward children throughout the early decades of the twentieth century, those meanings shifted and the bicycle became mostly an apolitical toy. During the Second World War, the suspension of automobile production, materials shortages, and oil-conservation measures generated a minor resurgence in everyday bicycle use throughout the U.S.— and everyday use of a bicycle became not just a practical choice but a symbolic expression of individual patriotism—only to give way to renewed focus on children's bicycles in the 1950s as suburbanization oriented around the private automobile intensified (Herlihy 2004).

During the 1960s and 1970s, the bicycle gained new associations as a political symbol, especially as a radical alternative to the environmental and experiential dilemmas facing modern society, and it is perhaps here where seeds for identifying bicycle transportation with "liberal" politics were planted. The greenways movement, also known as "rails-to-trails," had emerged around this time, with the goal of developing recreational and transportation pathways of scenic beauty. The greenways movement provided a connection for the bicycle—which was becoming popular again among adults during the "second bicycle boom"—to landscape preservation-oriented ecopolitics as local environmental groups around the country began advocating for the conversion of old rail lines and other degraded urban areas into bicycle paths.

An even more substantial force here was a shift in the environmental movement during the 1973–1974 oil crisis away from primarily landscape preservation concerns to accommodate anxieties over energy conservation and efficiency, poor air quality due to automobiles and industrial production, and the erosion of conviviality related to mass motorization (Horton 2006). One of the more strident voices in this period was Ivan Illich (1973), who articulated a critique of automobility in which he posited an inverse relationship between high energy consumption and social well-being. Illich rejected automobility as a form of "energy slavery," characterized by dependence on cheap petroleum, creeping reliance on technology in everyday life, the industrialization of traffic, and an emphasis on speed. He argued that in remaking modern transportation systems, "free people must travel the road to productive social relations at the speed of a bicycle" (1977: 118).

The symbolic association between the bicycle and critiques of industrial modernity and environmental degradation became solidly intertwined during this period, based on a perception that automobiles were driving affluent societies toward environmental apocalypse and that the use of the bicycle for everyday transportation could return society to ecological and social sanity (Horton 2006: 43). These ideas carried appeal beyond the arena of ecopolitics, and gained adherents among neighborhood activists, communitarians, anarchists, and others constructing "cultures of resistance" and non-consumption oriented lifestyles These groups, such as the New York City Anti-Automobile Alliance, often used antagonistic and theatrical means to draw attention to the environmental problems and threats to pedestrian well-being caused by automobiles, as well as the potential of the bicycle as a tool of everyday urban transportation (Furness 2010). As Horton (n.d.) observes, in these particular contexts, "the bicycle both symbolises and produces a desired compression of everyday life, fitting an expressive politics concerned with authenticity, community, and elevation of 'the local.'"

At the national and state levels, the small number of bicycle advocates similarly emphasized the transportation potential of bicycles. However, such radicalism was tempered if not altogether absent in their approaches to bike partisanship. The dominant approach of bicycle partisanship in the 1970s and 1980s was less associated with strident critiques of automobility than with efforts to gain legal status for bicycles as vehicles with the right to the road (Mapes 2009). The critical thrust of these efforts lay not in an outright rejection of the automobile but in advocating bicycle legislation based on symbolically defining the bicycle as the legal equivalent of an automobile, and developing a "share the road" ethic through the practice of what is called "Effective Cycling" (primarily known today as "Vehicular Cycling").

Under the influence of a transportation engineer, writer, and activist named John Forester, the practice of "Effective Cycling" was based on the dictum that "Cyclists fare best when they act and are treated as drivers of vehicles" (Forester 1977/2008:1). This practice required training and discipline in "driving" (not riding) a bicycle, a set of techniques for riding with automobile traffic that began to be taught (and continues to be taught) in bicycle skills courses throughout the country. Importantly, Forester, who was president of the League of American Bicyclists during the early 1980s, was an influential and outspoken voice against building bicycle infrastructure, such as bicycle lanes or trailways—for which there were few policy and funding mechanisms anyway during the 1970s and 1980s—viewing these special facilities as an erosion of bicycling's claim of equal rights to the road, and a needlessly divisive strategy that would alienate the vast majority of Americans who drive automobiles (Mapes 2009; Furness 2010).[2] The domination of the effective cycling paradigm had two important consequences for bicycle advocacy, one being that it offered an expedient way for public officials to avoid investing in bicycle infrastructure and programs, and the second, that the actual practice of effective cycling had a tendency to redefine urban cycling as a disciplined and elite practice—both of these were controversial then and continue to be debated within advocacy circles today, as explored in Box 4.1.

Box 4.1 Vehicular Cycling and the Politics of Inclusivity

To someone who has been trained to drive an automobile, the practice of Vehicular Cycling (VC) makes intuitive sense. It emphasizes that cyclists need to ride on the road in harmony with other vehicle traffic and follow all of its rules, including moving in the direction of traffic flow, respecting all signals and signs, positioning oneself to make left turns near the center line, being clear about one's intention to change lanes, and riding on the right side of the lane only when it is convenient and safe for the cyclist, not necessarily because motorists are backing up behind and getting impatient. It asserts that cyclists should confidently "take the lane" when conditions warrant it, negotiate with motorists as required, and always be predictable to other road users to avoid collisions. VC offers a coherent and empowering set of skills for navigating urban traffic, and its principles exist in some shape or form at the heart of all traffic skills trainings offered by bicycle advocacy organizations.

At the same time, VC has long been a highly divisive issue among cyclists. Critics have charged that its proponents are too rigid and dogmatic and that VC gives in too readily to an automobile-centered transportation system. Further, the practice condemns cyclists to sit in traffic jams with automobiles by divesting the bicycle of its ability to get through hold-ups through creative use of street space (Hurst 2006). Some critical commentators also charge that cyclists, who are doing less damage to the earth and urban environments, should take the privilege of bypassing cars because they are the ones who are "doing good" (Schwartz 2010). These criticisms focus on the contexts and practices of actually riding a bicycle in urban traffic, but a different kind of criticism has been gaining traction that targets VC's political rejection of special facilities and on-road treatments for cyclists. Some of this criticism emerges from awareness that countries with high rates of cycling, such as the Netherlands, have developed special infrastructure for cyclists, as well as the increasing involvement of urban and transportation planners in bicycle issues whose professional orientation (quite naturally) emphasizes the design of infrastructure to suit specific transportation needs.

In this context, a number of scholars and activists have sought to explicitly reframe VC as promoting a form of social injustice and exclusivity. As a pair of influential bicycle transportation planners recently argued,

> In the vehicular cycling model, cyclists must constantly evaluate traffic, looking back, signaling, adjusting lateral position and speed, sometimes blocking a lane and sometimes yielding, always trying to fit into the 'dance' that is traffic. Research shows that most people feel very unsafe engaging in this kind of dance, in which a single mistake could be fatal. Children as well as many women and elders are excluded. While some people, especially young men, may find the challenge stimulating, it is stressful and unpleasant for the vast majority.
>
> (Pucher and Buehler 2009: 62–63)

They follow up with a powerful question: "Do we really want to restrict cycling to a tiny percentage of the population and exclude most women, children, and seniors? Or should we be truly inclusive and design our cycling policies for everyone?" (Pucher and Buehler 2009: 63). Bicycle scholar Zack Furness (2010) has taken these criticisms a step further and charges that VC is not only elitist and exclusionary, but cynically exploits a civil rights language of "equal rights" to serve a small number of cyclists.

The League of American Bicyclists recently experienced a deep rift over what some members perceived as a slighting of VC, and a rival offshoot organization was formed whose primary goal is to protect and promote VC principles. Moving beyond the acrimonious nature of these squabbles, what is at issue here are distinct political visions, moral meanings, and physical practices around several big questions:

- Who should be an urban cyclist?
- What constitutes acceptable risk or safety for an urban cyclist?
- What responsibilities and bodily practices are assumed necessary for using a bicycle as a form of urban transportation?
- What are the primary ways to foster inclusivity in cycling?

Largely because bicycle advocacy has been white and middle class, questions about inclusivity and privilege have played a minimal role in the bike movement. It is just beginning to grapple with these difficult and unresolved questions.

Opportunities for Reflection and Action

For understanding the practice of VC, it is useful to go right to the source, John Forester's website (http://www.johnforester.com/), book (http://mitpress.mit.edu/catalog/item/default.asp?ttype=2&tid=5650), or this lecture where he articulates some key principles: http://video.google.ca/videoplay?docid=-6082181397382918705&ei=gmlGS4CMJ6qBlge57LXSDw&q=john+forester&hl=en#.

Bike Forums has a lively, and at times shockingly polarizing, forum for discussing and debating Vehicular Cycling: http://www.bikeforums.net/forumdisplay.php/252-Vehicular-Cycling-%28VC%29. Numerous bloggers have engaged critically on the topic, such as here: http://www.ibiketo.ca/blog/2010/04/26/politics-safety-and-vehicular-cycling. As you read through these, pay close attention to how each might answer the questions posed above.

During the 1990s, a host of factors created a turn-around in what had become a moribund and divided cause (Mapes 2009). In the late 1980s, a coalition promoting alternative transportation interests—among them the national Rails to Trails advocacy group and the Bicycling Federation of America—came together to lobby for federal transportation dollars, out of which they had traditionally been locked. Their watershed moment came with the passage of the 1991 federal transportation bill (called ISTEA), legislation that mandated the federal government to support the development of bicycle transportation projects and laid a foundation for it to provide grant funding for bike projects to states, which it began to do in subsequent transportation bills throughout the 1990s and 2000s. The unexpected rise in popularity of the mountain bike in the 1980s had also revived the bicycle industry's fortunes, and it became apparent to some manufacturers that lobbying for access to public lands and for broader federal support for cycling was important to the industry's future. The lobbying arm of the bike industry, known today as Bikes Belong, began dedicating substantial funding to advocacy efforts. With prospects for the bike cause looking up, representatives of fifteen national and state bicycle advocacy groups made a major decision in the mid-1990s to join together and coordinate their lobbying and advocacy efforts, calling their relationship the Thunderhead Alliance. They soon renamed it the Alliance for Biking and Walking, which itself is now a stand-alone national organization that provides over 200 member state and local advocacy groups with training in how to organize bicycle advocacy campaigns. The development of this capacity-building organization has been viewed as a critical step in the maturation of the bicycle cause.

With these efforts gaining a head of steam, during the past few years some bicycle advocates have begun to refer, perhaps with a detectable sense of self-awareness but at the same time with increasing confidence, to their efforts to promote the bicycle as a "social movement." This identification as a social movement in itself should be understood as a manifestation of the flexibility of the bicycle as a political symbol. Such language connotes a popular struggle to make political and social change from the bottom up, emphasizing the autonomy and coherence of the bicycle cause itself over the bicycle serving the causes of other social movements, such as environmentalism or anti-automobile urban resistance cultures. This reframing of the bicycle cause as an autonomous issue has become especially critical as bicycle advocates have developed close associations with government (from city to state and federal levels) to pressure for dedicated bicycle infrastructure and program funding, to try to influence transportation policy, and to collaborate in the design and implementation of actual programs and projects. But as is apparent at the National Bike Summit, the lines between popular movement and government can blur as prominent politicians, city officials, and others in the public sector have joined, or at least articulated their support for, the bicycle cause.

Given the range of symbolic positionings and political meanings the bike movement has inherited and continues to generate, numerous niches and fronts have emerged that hold distinct ideological stances and concrete political strategies to promote the everyday use of bicycles. Among these are those seeking policy changes (often referred to as the "policy wonks"), manufacturers and retailers, community and neighborhood activists, recreationalists and fitness advocates, ride organizers, transportation planners, educators, Critical Mass-type instigators, do-it-yourself anarchists, and others—each of whom carries specific perspectives about the role of the bicycle as a force for change, how to position it symbolically and practically, even whether or not they are "advocates" (connoting a type of social and political reform) or "activists" (connoting the promotion of radical change). These actors do not always interact directly with each other and they occupy distinct political arenas and realms of social action, suggesting that the bike movement, such as it is, exists less as a coherent or united force for change than a dynamic social and political arena in its own right where basic issues—especially the role of the bicycle in generating social change—remain unsettled. This situation can produce important dilemmas and conflicting visions within the movement.

As the next two sections explore, these dilemmas and conflicting visions are especially appreciable at the local scale of Burlington, Vermont. In these sections, I focus on two arenas of cultural politics—distinct perspectives on the strategic importance of the bicycle's visibility in the movement, and distinct perspectives over how to get more people interested in everyday bicycling when investing in infrastructure and programs is not a high public-sector priority—to demonstrate the heterogeneous and contextual ways bicycle advocacy takes shape.

Asserting the Visibility (and Invisibility) of the Bicycle

"If there's one central principle I want to share with you today, it's be visible!" explained Ted, who was running a bicycle commuter workshop in Burlington. He went on, "Most people assume that with commuting it's all about the bike, and everything else is an afterthought. But I'm going to begin with the stuff that makes you visible, because unless you're riding on a bike path you want to be as visible as you possibly can with cars." Ted proceeded to talk through how being visible is a means to reduce the risks associated with commuting by bicycle, and he periodically drew objects from a nearby table to demonstrate useful tools in the quest for visibility—blinking rear lights, helmet lights, gloves with LED lights on them, handlebar lights, and, his tour-de-force, a neon yellowish-green jacket. As he said to mild snickering, "Don't fear day-glo! There are too many drivers out there talking on cell phones."

In this bicycle commuter workshop, framing bicycle mobility by downplaying the bike itself and playing up the visibility of the rider was cast as a purely pragmatic concern. But the more involved I've become with bicycle advocacy through ethnographic research, the more I've come to understand that there is a deeper level of nuance and important symbolic politics in incitements to be visible, because visibility draws attention not just to the individual cyclist but to the activity of bicycling and, potentially, to it as a socio-political cause. One of the reasons advocates hold bicycle commuter workshops is not just to share practical advice but to get more people on the roads using bicycles. Their motivations are based on the "safety in numbers" principle, the so-called "virtuous cycle" in which as their numbers grow, the risks to individual cyclists diminish as motorists become more accustomed to seeing bicycles on the roads (Blue 2010). More importantly, having more people on the streets helps legitimize the practice of everyday bicycle mobility itself. It is not far from this idea to the notion that the solitary cyclist is doing something more than "just" riding a bike—that the act of riding a bicycle for a practical purpose is invested with socio-political meaning. Indeed, I've heard on multiple occasions a version of the following (as recounted to me by a Burlington bicycle advocate): "Becoming a transportation cyclist makes you an advocate. As one more rider, you help make the rest of us safer, and you become more aware and invested in making change on the streets."

At the same time, however, the politics of visibility are flexible, and there are in fact important variations in, and disagreements about, efforts to symbolically position the bicycle in order to communicate an advocacy message. While some prioritize making the bicycle itself highly visible, others (such as Ted) seek to downplay it. These are not simply tactical matters, but often reflect deeper philosophical differences surrounding the role of the bicycle in everyday life, as well as how to legitimize that role symbolically so that others will recognize it. As an illustration, consider the contrast between one family's practice of promoting the bicycle's visibility as a form of everyday activism and environmental values, and the ways one of the local bicycle advocacy groups deemphasizes the bicycle so as to not alienate potential allies to their cause of building a broader movement for active recreation and transportation.

Carl, Leslie, and their two kids, aged six and nine, practice everyday bicycle mobility. For them, emphasizing the visibility of the bicycle itself offers a means to communicate a pro-bicycle message and a daily reflection of the family's commitment to individual environmental responsibility. One reflection of this commitment happens almost every morning throughout the school year, as Carl and the kids mount a large, brightly colored three-wheeled cycle for their ride to school. Carl pedals while the kids sit behind him on top of a large flatbed like you might see on a truck. The kids are used to riding—they even like it, at least when it's not raining or snowing because it is, as Carl notes, "like a big convertible"—and their family has been getting around by bicycle for as long as they remember. Carl built the tricycle himself, and its unconventional—somewhat unfinished and recycled—looks turn a lot of heads, which the kids like too. At the speed they ride and with the openness of the cycle itself, they draw a lot of attention to themselves and have plenty of opportunities to salute friends and passersby.

The family owns a relatively new car but they might use it only once or twice a week, usually for trips of ten miles or more. They have made a deliberate decision to organize their lives around principles of simplicity and localism: eating locally produced foods, creatively recycling things to avoid buying new items, and spending their money when they can in local businesses. They view bicycles and their cycle truck as playing an indispensable role in constructing this kind of life. Neither Carl nor Leslie holds a formal role in any bicycle advocacy group, but Carl in particular is closely connected to other cyclists and the city's small community of bicycle builders, attends bike-related events and activities in the community when he can, and has participated in various mass rides, including Critical Mass. As mentioned above, this kind of individual orientation and initiative is often viewed as something more consequential than simply being an individual choice, and the idea that the everyday use of a bicycle itself can be a form of activism circulates widely, a notion Carl accepts: "Yes, I guess I do think of myself as an activist when it comes to bicycles."

Although Carl and Leslie both view their commitment to daily bicycling as an expression of their shared values and as part of a bigger cause, they nevertheless have differing views of bicycles and bicycling between themselves. From an early age, Carl has viewed bicycles as intrinsically interesting machines, embraced the physical act of riding a bicycle, and has long considered himself a "cyclist," a unique identity based prioritizing the bicycle in one's lifestyle. But the meanings he attaches to bicycles and riding them are complex, and have changed over the years. Initially, as Carl explains, "It was my ticket to freedom. It allowed me to do things that I normally wouldn't do, and I was attracted to the physical experience of riding a bicycle. Only later on did it change from something fun to something like, 'Oh wow, the bicycle is one of the most useful tools ever made.'" Carl's first job was working as a building inspector with a specialty in energy efficiency, and he explains that his perspective on the bicycle began changing because of that work:

Here I am doing energy efficiency work and I end up driving two hours across the state to do an inspection on a building to see if something is done properly. And I begin feeling, "Ooh, think about the fuel I'm using to do this, and all the embodied fuel in the car itself." How much energy did we really save after all is said and done? The numbers have been run. That feeling of frustration is one of the things I got sick of about doing energy efficiency work. Once I moved on to a different profession, I got rid of the car. I didn't want it anymore . . .

We have a car again, but nowadays, part of me is affronted by thought that I'm going to start up an internal combustion engine, heat it up, move thousands of pounds of car with me to go eight miles away, or five miles, or two miles away. And it's like "Arrghh, no!" But I also get pure enjoyment out of riding a bicycle. Sometimes it's hard to distinguish between, "Am I taking the bicycle because it's fun, or is it because I feel so strongly about the environmental reasons for doing it?"

Leslie, whose ideas of bicycling do not carry the same connotations of physical pleasure, views bicycles primarily in terms of their instrumental value. She does not think of herself as a "cyclist" but as someone who uses a bicycle to get around, the bicycle in her mind representing a form of inexpensive and (usually, but not always) convenient short-distance transportation that aligns well with her broad commitment to simple living.

Visiting Carl and Leslie's house, one is immediately struck by the proliferation of bicycles on the porch, in the yard, and in the garage. Carl observes the family owns 13 bicycles, only five or six of which are in operating condition at any one time. He "cannibalizes" parts from some to keep others in working order, and has just built a whole new bicycle by combining parts from several. For Carl, working on bicycles directly—maintaining them in working order, recycling parts between them—is an expression of creativity and a chance work on tangible, mechanical things that does not happen in his new work as a computer programmer. He has also been drawn to designing and welding his own frames out of steel tubing, one result being his unique "cycle truck" described above. In explaining these activities, Carl views them through a lens of his environmental commitment, based on explicitly recognizing a distinction between the practice of bicycle riding and the material object itself. As he observes, "Even if I'm not adding to global warming by riding my bike, the bike itself still has an environmental cost, in the steel bearings, the rubber in the tires, the steel or aluminum in the frame, the oil in the chain. It's a polluting, global industry. It's the magnitude of the impact that makes it different from a car. But it still has an environmental impact that I worry about."

For Carl, any uncritical notion of the bicycle as an environmentally virtuous vehicle is suspect, and his commitment to cannibalizing bikes and do-it-yourselfism reflects not just an appreciation for the materiality of the bicycle itself, but also a way of visibly demonstrating some level of accountability and responsibility to the environmental dimensions of his relationship with the bicycle that he does not necessarily see in the industry itself. (For deeper background on this perspective, see Box 4.2.) For Carl and his close associates and friends who share his interest in bicycle building, there is something subversive yet honest and powerful about putting a recycled or self-built bicycle out front and center—making it as visible as possible with bright paint, regular use on the streets, and so on—which in his mind is a key strategy to draw attention to pedal power as a viable form of getting around the city, and a symbol of one's commitment to environmental responsibility that just riding any bicycle doesn't necessarily achieve on its own.

Box 4.2 The Bicycle and Dilemmas of Sustainability

As Carl's perspectives on bicycles and their ecological impacts suggest, not everyone takes the relationship between bicycling and sustainability at face value. Indeed, the notion of an "environmental paradox" (Ulrich 2006) involved in bicycling threatens to disrupt any certainties on the subject. One set of concerns revolves around a hypothetical argument that whatever reductions in emissions and particulate matter bicycles generate vis-à-vis automobiles could be canceled out over the long term by the health benefits of bicycling, that will lead to longer lives and extend the resource-intensive consumer lifestyles of urban cyclists over a longer period (Ulrich 2006; Stein 2006). Largely because it could be read as a defense of automobility, relies on vaguely defined order of magnitude effects, and defines the bicycle solely through a reductionistic emissions-centered framework, this argument has failed to gain much traction among those concerned about the connections between bicycling and sustainability.

A more powerful set of concerns takes a more holistic perspective on the bicycle itself, focusing on the practices of the bicycle industry and the life cycle of a mass-produced bicycle from its origins in raw materials to the end of its life (Ryan and Durning 1997). These concerns are expressed by Rosen (2002) in the following way: while cycling is part of the sustainability agenda, sustainability does not seem to be too important in the bicycle industry's agenda. For example, while major bicycle companies such as Wisconsin-based Trek have declared their corporate commitment to sustainability, such claims typically focus on how headquarters offices practice energy efficiency, recycle goods, promote non-automobile transportation among their employees, etc. Away from corporate headquarters, where 60 percent of bicycles are produced, the actual processes of bicycle manufacturing are dirty, resource-intensive, and occur in countries that have lax environmental standards (Edwards 2011). The industry's reorganization from mass production centralized in particular U.S. and European companies during the twentieth century to one based on globally dispersed flexible specialization beginning in the 1980s, has raised new concerns about the environmental and social consequences of now global-scale bicycle manufacturing.

As explored in Chapter 2, the parts that make up the typical mass-produced bicycle involve raw materials and a decentralized network of producers, suppliers, and laborers from numerous locations around the globe. The fact that these arrangements and the processes involved in them are fundamentally opaque—for example, the identifiable names on a bicycle part may be nothing more than the brand name of the company that distributes the part or assembled the final product—generates uncertainty and suspicion, even unsettling moral concerns over the "ecological footprint" of the globally produced bicycle (though actually calculating it, given the opaqueness of the industry, is difficult). Another concern revolves around a logic central to the industry, of producing goods that will quickly become obsolete. In addition, the production of repairable parts and components has been in decline, as major contemporary component manufacturers like Shimano produce components that are designed to be replaced, not repaired by users (Rosen 2002). Responding to these concerns and testing the limits of bicycle sustainability discourse, there has been growing interest in developing bicycles from renewable resources like bamboo, which can be useful for making bicycle frames (Furness 2010).

What is striking about these concerns, perhaps, is not necessarily their broad acceptance across cycling publics or within mainstream sustainable transportation discourses. In these settings, the bicycle's contributions to sustainability are appealing because they maximize certain efficiencies or because, quite simply, they are not automobiles. Rather, what is striking here is that these concerns about the bicycle's ecological footprint mark a fundamental ambivalence about the bicycle's association with industrial modernity that one can see lurking throughout the history of the bicycle and its relationship with the environment and ecopolitics (Rosen 2002; Freudendahl-Pedersen 2009; Furness 2010). Whether it is as an escape to nature from urban civilization, an antidote to an automobile-centered environmental apocalypse, or expressing a holistic view of the intertwined economic, ecological, and social dimensions of transportation, the bicycle is a product of the very industrial contexts from which at least some of its users have sought to distance themselves.

Across the city from Carl and Leslie's neighborhood is the non-profit membership organization Local Motion, a 1,000 household membership organization, whose mission is to promote "people-powered transportation and recreation for healthy and sustainable communities." It is similarly concerned with the visibility of the bicycle, although in different ways. Established just over a decade ago, it is the organization that coordinates the Safe Streets Collaborative and its Intersection Actions. It also provides recreational cyclists with maps of local greenways, rents bicycles to visiting tourists, organizes fun rides for its members, holds bicycle commuter workshops for residents, runs a community bike shop for low-income residents, and plays technical consulting and advocacy roles in city, county, and state government, promoting policies and infrastructure that make walking and bicycling safer and more convenient. It enjoys credibility and high name recognition in the city and the broader region where it has been devoting a lot of attention recently, and its mission has evolved beyond bicycle issues into pedestrian advocacy and promoting other forms of what it calls "active transportation."

In the past couple of years, Local Motion has won several high-profile victories in its political advocacy work, including getting city officials to reduce the city's speed limit to 25 mph and a Complete Streets resolution, which requires the city to plan and design road projects that are safe and accessible for all users, not just automobiles. Yet the organization's primary public profile is for its promotion of active leisure and everyday recreation. It is especially known for its advocacy work in developing and expanding the city's lakefront bike path. Indeed, its early formation as a non-profit membership organization was focused on achieving an extension of the bike path, first by providing weekend ferry service across a river mouth at the northern end of the path to allow cyclists to continue into the neighboring town, and then a successful lobbying and fundraising campaign for the creation of a permanent bridge over the river. This close symbolic association with the bike path and recreational cycling has attracted a membership that is primarily recreation-oriented, and at the same time has led to disconnection or weak ties with individuals like Carl and Leslie (who are not members) who view the organization's privileging of recreation as marginal to their primary concern of using the bicycle for moving around the city and as an expression of their desire to "live simply."

This focus on recreation and the development of a greenway is viewed within the organization through a "sustainability" lens, as promoting non-motorized leisure activities and getting people outside to enjoy beautiful landscapes. As one of the staff has explained to me, the emphasis on recreation is also strategically central to the organization's mission of building a broader movement for active and sustainable transportation, since a recreational paradigm can be used as a non-controversial, "soft" way to pull a wider public into a different way of thinking about their own everyday transportation habits. As he says, "recreation pulls them in, and we hope it will get people to move toward active and sustainable transportation."

That "soft" approach extends to the ways the organization relates to government agencies and transportation planning officials. "We aren't 'shout-and-carry-signs' advocates," observes one staffer, adding "Figuring out where the common ground is and getting people together is our goal. Our identity is as a partner. We build bridges and get things done, as opposed to organization that prevents bad things from happening, like some environmental groups. You can't do both. If you're going to take the approach of stopping things like every road project without bike lanes, you'll piss off powerful interests." That non-confrontational, collaborative approach with government institutions has won Local Motion numerous consulting grants from the state, county, and city to provide technical input on bicycle and pedestrian policies and transportation plans. It also means that when it does try to mobilize cyclists around an issue, Local Motion exercises what one of its staffers termed "quiet advocacy," such as a recent situation when the city wasn't following through on finalizing a Complete Streets demonstration project.[3] Behind the scenes and without drawing attention to itself, so as not to alienate its partners in city government and Public Works (the department in charge of implementing the project), Local Motion quietly organized almost two hundred cyclists to write letters of support for the project and the city followed through on the project.

These positionings reflect the blurred lines between the organization's identity as an advocacy group pressuring for change from the outside and its role as an insider consultant serving a government client, which can create certain dilemmas for staffers. As a staffer observes, "One question we grapple with quite a bit is how do you harness the power of a subversive movement to mainstream issues where we are? It's like a judo move. A good portion of the energy in the bike movement is not where we are in the mainstream." In grappling with that question, Local Motion has developed a complex relationship with the bicycle. Although most of its staffers are themselves everyday transportation cyclists and the organization periodically organizes fun rides through the city and surrounding countryside, an influential staffer explains, "We have to always remember that we're so much more than bicycles. We have to balance our work and identity with the concerns of walkers and other people who are active. We also don't want to 'reclaim the streets' for the bike in such a way that it loses those people who are primarily interested in recreation." It is this second statement that is especially important: one of the fears here is that bicycles can be viewed as confrontational—particularly by many automobile users who feel they disrupt the flow of traffic—which could end up alienating potential allies in the broader cause of getting people moving toward active and sustainable transportation.

Reflected in Local Motion's approach to advocacy is an ambivalence about a particular image of the bicycle as a fringe vehicle, an image that is even threatening to an automobile-centered status quo if it is pushed too hard. It is sensitive to the idea that cyclists are a minority—and in Burlington, a minority in relation to pedestrians of whom there are greater numbers. As a result, staffers often strategically downplay the bicycle, especially when anti-bicycle voices in the media and government are strong, "shifting," as one staffer in the organization noted to me one day, "to pedestrian issues as the political winds blow against bicycles." A striking reflection of this approach toward bicycles, of strategically keeping them in the background, lies in the recommendation of a visiting active transportation advocate who was invited to engage staffers in critical reflection on their work, when he said:

> Don't talk about bicycles. You'll alienate a lot of people who see them as anti-automobile, or just don't like cyclists. You should talk about the importance of greenways and scenic beauty. You should talk about the importance of public health and obesity reduction. Those things are much more palatable for a lot of people and politically-acceptable for politicians. And then at the end, when you get down to concrete ways to bring those things together, you introduce the bicycle into the picture as the vehicle that can unite these two interests. The bicycle will benefit from all this, but it can't be about the bicycle itself.

In this view—which the advocate termed "giving it away to get it back"—the bicycle's virtues lie in its supporting role in promoting mostly non-controversial practices, such as the creation of public parks and greenways, or ideals of healthy living. As a result, as one staffer explained, "In our advocacy we are beginning to align ourselves with obesity prevention plans, and school physical education classes, and we try to quietly slip the bicycle into them." This quiet work is justified primarily because it is intended to expand the notion of active and sustainable mobility to a wider public that does not, nor probably ever will, think of itself as "cyclists." The idea of bicycle advocacy here, perhaps ironically, ends up removing the bicycle from the foreground.

Dilemmas of Fun and Convenience

In Burlington, the cultural politics of bicycle advocacy are not simply concerned with the symbolic framing and visibility of the bicycle itself, but also with the practical social actions necessary to generate a commitment to the everyday use of bicycles, to convert those who otherwise might hop into a car to consider going by bicycle. The focus here is less on concerns over how the bicycle itself should be seen and presented—although these are seen as a complementary issue—and more on what practical actions will mobilize and motivate people around the activity of bicycling itself.

As discussed in Chapter 3, there is a strong sense of unfufilled promise among bicycle advocates and bicyclists in Burlington regarding lack of follow-through with city transportation plans that prioritize the consolidation and improvement of a bicycle network. They often argue that the inconsistency in the network makes the activity of bicycling on city streets seem risky, dangerous, or inconvenient. The basic problem here is that when the city's commitment to major infrastructure improvement is stagnant—and the "build-it-and-they-will-come" logic of bicycle planning is getting nowhere—a distinct set of strategies needs to be developed to get more people bicycling, based on the hope that the city will be forced to deliver on its plans either because the sheer number of people on bicycles is too much for the current infrastructure, or that with a broader base of everyday cyclists more people might begin to clamor for change.

Not surprisingly, how to actually get more people bicycling can generate sharp discussion and debate. One common set of approaches circulates around the idea of cultivating an association of bicycling with fun and good times. From an advocacy point of view, this approach has numerous merits because it can generate enthusiasm and open pocketbooks to increase donations. It is a long-standing strategy of mainstream advocacy groups like Local Motion, reflected not just in its organization of "fun rides" for its members but in its distribution of free stickers meant to communicate a lighthearted message: "Put Some Fun Between Your Legs!," "Spoke Bloke," or "Ride Like A Girl." As one staffer observed, "We consciously try to cultivate fun. You have to promote change through the heart instead of the head. For years we've been saying biking is great and we have lots of rational arguments for it. But what seems to move people is the pleasure-seeking part of the brain." This approach is based on a practical appreciation of the American view of bicycling as a recreational and leisure activity. One of the limitations implicit in this approach, however, is that it doesn't address how to bridge the gap between the idea that riding a bicycle is enjoyable, and the practical reality of riding in stressful conditions of urban traffic—the actual context of everyday bicycle use in Burlington—which is not necessarily "fun" for a lot of people.

The broader point here is that "fun" can mean different things to different people, generating competing visions of what is a "fun" way to get people interested in bicycling or to induce them to use a bicycle more often for everyday purposes. Promoting the "fun" of bicycling was a central goal of a short-lived "biketivist" group that emerged and then dissolved during the course of my fieldwork. Calling itself the Burlington Bicycle Coalition (BBC), the loose-knit coalition was organized around a core of young men and women who, like Carl and Leslie, identify closely with the bicycle as a tool and expression of a sustainable, local lifestyle. They were driven by a sense of frustration that mainstream bicycle advocates in Burlington—among them Local Motion and the city's own bicycle advisory committee, the Burlington Bike/Walk Council— were not moving quickly enough to make "real change" in conditions for cyclists on the streets. They also wanted to recognize and nurture Burlington's "bicycle culture"—not in the anthropological sense as I've used it in this book, but in the sense of a creative, arts and crafts scene oriented around bicycles—as a new center of political and social energy around bicycles. At the heart of these expressions was both a sense of alienation from mainstream bicycle advocacy, whose profile is older, upper-middle class, and recreation-oriented, and a belief that a new kind of more socially inclusive bike movement could emerge with a stronger political and social identity.

Along these lines the coalition started organizing bike-themed movie showings, put together a neighborhood bike tool station free to users, encouraged the production and exchange of bike-themed crafts and jewelry made with recycled bike parts, and began hosting its own "fun rides" throughout the city, such as costumed rides, full moon rides, bike messenger-style Alley Cat races, and others. These events attracted mostly younger riders and families similar in profile and outlook to the BBC's organizers, which is to say, looking for fun experiences and community. Nevertheless, the rides in particular were influenced by a Critical Mass-inspired notion that a sustained presence of large numbers of cyclists on the streets would communicate a strong political message to motorists and city officials about the enthusiasm and strength of the bicycle-riding community. Representatives of the group also started showing up at more traditional venues of bicycle advocacy, such as bicycle-related events and workshops put on by groups like Local Motion, and their clear impatience with the pace of change, as well as their defiant approach on the streets, began to increase tensions. Those tensions culminated in an afternoon "meet up" of the city's bicycle and pedestrian advocacy groups, where as one organizer explained "Too many groups in the city right now claim to be about bikes. We need to figure out how to work together." Not much concrete came of the meet-up—it was more of a chance to begin rebuilding relationships between advocates whose relations were strained—and not long after, the group more or less dissolved as some of its key organizers moved away from Burlington.

In the aftermath of the BBC's dissolution, one of its organizers, a young woman who worked as a bicycle mechanic, observed, "We wanted to present the bicycle as a fun and positive thing, but we also wanted to push the envelope. You know, it pissed some people off." Some of this tension was around the distinctive brand of "fun" the BBC cultivated, including Critical Mass-like tactics of riding through stop signs and taking up lanes of traffic. Tensions also centered around the fact that the BBC organized itself as an assertion of youth-oriented identity politics intended to challenge the mainstream framing of bicycling fun as a recreational and apolitical pursuit of "old people." In the end, it was difficult for the BBC to sustain the oppositional energy and coherence they sought to develop. Expanding on the dissolution of the coalition, the young woman concluded: "You also can't just keep doing fun rides and fun social activities. People lose interest. They move on to other things. It didn't offer a consistent politics." Which is not to say that some of the rides are not still being organized, or that bicycle-related arts and crafts have disappeared—if anything, they've been increasingly viewed as hip. These things have continued, in spite of the BBC's dissolution, which suggests more than anything, perhaps, that the BBC was a brief collective expression of a set of ideas for promoting bicycling that are rooted in a political philosophy of decentralized and organic social action that is understood to wax and wane.

During this same period, a radically different idea about how to promote the activity of cycling in Burlington was coalescing around a paradigm of the decidedly not-fun but rather mundane issue of making bicycling more convenient by providing new bike parking facilities. Headed by a pair of long-time bicycle advocates working more or less independently (at least initially) of any single advocacy group, the focus of the initiative was not on getting more bicycle racks for the city—the city has an ordinance that governs that issue anyway—but about providing safe and secure bicycle parking at special events such as concerts, community lectures, and Saturday farmers' markets. The actual practice involves setting up a bounded corral-like space near an event where a volunteer attendant receives the bicycle, helps park it on a modified rack, and keeps an eye on it until its owner returns when the event is finished. After several years of doing "demonstration projects," the initiative has picked up steam and there are now dozens of events in the city during the year that promise secure parking, drawing on a cadre of volunteers who get credit at the local food coop for helping out.

The advocacy goal here was to change people's meanings and expectations of what bicycle parking could be and address several commonly heard reasons given by people for not riding their bikes in the city: that their bicycle could get stolen, that there is not enough parking especially when a lot of people are attending the same event, or that it is inconvenient to have to find parking far from the event itself when bike racks are full. As Mike, one of the organizers, shared with me in an interview:

> This bike parking thing, it's so logical. I mean, you get in your car and you drive somewhere and you know you're going to be able to park. A bike can certainly park anywhere, but is it safe? As bikes have become more expensive you want security. I've talked to people who say first thing they did when they got their bike was paint it black and make it look like a street bike. They don't want to let people know it's a good bike which is so antithetical to the way we treat our cars.

The initiative was also based on a distinct vision of advocacy, of (as he explained) "what can *we* do for *you?* Usually it's the reverse for advocates. It's what can *you* do to advance *our* mission?" Emphasizing the fundamentally mundane nature of people's interests, Bill, a local bike builder who was working with Mike on the initiative, observed, "It seems like sometimes we do everything possible to avoid the obvious. People believe that unless you do something that costs millions of dollars, it will never work. The parking thing is really basic, but it doesn't draw a lot of attention among many advocates because it's not especially sexy."

The idea of secure bicycle parking had been kicking around for at least 20 years between Mike—who had once traveled to Oregon and was introduced to a community bike shop where the young people working there in a job-training program raised money by parking bicycles at city events—and Bill, who had traveled to the Netherlands and learned of the Dutch system of secure bicycle parking, one version of which is a storefront where bicycles can be kept under the watchful eye of an attendant. The primary catalyst for moving forward came a couple of years ago when Local Motion invited a national group, the Alliance for Biking and Walking, to conduct a workshop on developing and winning bicycle and pedestrian advocacy campaigns. Mike and Bill attended the workshop, which provided them with a methodology on how to proceed and several uninterrupted days to plan what they now envisioned as an advocacy "campaign." Explaining the approach they learned there, Mike observed:

> It's a process of deconstruction. You take what your end goal is going to be. Our end goal is to get secure bike parking as a requirement for all special events in the city. How do you do that? You get it as a city ordinance that requires it at all big public events. But then how do you get an ordinance? You get political support in the City Council. How do you get City Council to back it? Well, you do a demonstration and get signatures. That's good for maybe the first year, but then you have to get a lot of backing. If you're going to park bikes, you're gonna need insurance.

The campaign is currently in what Mike refers to as "the political stage," which is winning City Council approval for an ordinance by lobbying individual councilors. The actual day-to-day operations of providing parking for events have been handed over to Local Motion staff and interns, not without a certain amount of uneasiness on the part of Bill and Mike—who fear it could "get swallowed" up within the bigger organization—but they viewed it as necessary to get the organization's insurance coverage. Nevertheless, they remain intimately involved in organizing volunteers, arranging for the purchase of equipment for the corral, and helping set up and take down the corral, which, as Mike observes "you often spend more time doing than actually parking bikes."

The bicycle parking campaign has been, according to these individuals and volunteers involved in it, arduous and mundane work that involves thinking through and managing many technical and logistical details. It reflects a dimension of bicycle advocacy that is quite distant from the (overly romantic) vision of organizing defiant and energetic groups of people to get on bicycles and roll through stop signs for a subversive good time, a perspective to bicycle advocacy Mike in particular has called "stupid" because it is so confrontational.

But the bicycle parking initiative has generated certain kinds of dilemmas of its own, one of the main ones being around how to get people excited about parking bicycles: as Mike observed, "without volunteers getting credit at the coop for food, we'd be sunk!" Furthermore, there is a fine line between appearing to be servile and building a broader collective cause of which the bicycle parking initiative is one expression. As Mike explained, "I fought hard against calling it valet parking. There's a subservience in its connotation. Secure bike parking assumes you've got to do something, you're part of the actual process of parking the bike. It's not hand it over and somebody will take care of it." The deeper issue here is that framing bicycle advocacy through a practice of addressing an issue of convenience doesn't necessarily engage people beyond the act of meeting a particular need at a particular moment, or alternatively, it requires a tangible incentive like volunteers receive from a cooperating food coop. Unlike the BBC's approach, which was to build collective energy around oppositional identity politics which can (at least temporarily) energize people to get on bikes, this approach is based on individuals interacting over a service one provides to another, and the potential for collective action is minimal.

Conclusion

One of Burlington's bicycle advocates once told me during an interview that "The contest for us is not just policies and striping on the roads, it is, at a fundamental level, over meanings." What I think he meant is that being an advocate involves the work of changing peoples' meanings about how they get around, which is mainly by car. The dual goal is to redefine the car as the source of certain societal and individual problems, and to introduce the bicycle as a solution to those problems.

I don't think he necessarily was referring to "the contest over meanings" as being primarily one that takes place within the community of people devoted to promoting greater everyday use of bicycles. Nevertheless, one of the reasons this chapter has framed the description and analysis of the bike movement as an arena of cultural politics is that there *is* a contest of meanings taking place within the movement. As this chapter has shown, bicycle advocacy has long been the context for the flexible use of symbolism and the contestation of meanings, both of which can generate numerous and sometimes conflicting strategies for social action.

And that dynamism very much continues today in Burlington. Consider, for example, the divergent perspectives described above on the visibility of the bicycle. On one level, the politics of the bicycle's visibility exposes distinct ideologies about the bicycle itself—from Carl's notion that the object itself deserves serious attention by working on it directly and understanding its environmental dimensions versus Local Motion's perspective that views the bicycle simply as a means to an end, which is a healthier and happier population. On another level, there is a deeper set of philosophical differences playing out between Carl and his family's everyday advocacy and Local Motion's strategic downplaying of the bicycle in order to win over people to active recreation and transportation. A major difference here has to do with the scale to which one's energy gets focused, from the hyper-localism and dwelling-in-place apparent in Carl and Leslie's vision of everyday bicycle use, to extending the bicycle's appeal to a broader polity while keeping the bicycle hidden or abstract in Local Motion's efforts. Can they be conjoined to a common agenda? Perhaps, but in fact there is a kind of mutual indifference at work: Carl and Leslie have avoided membership in Local Motion based on the idea that it is not politically edgy enough and does not fully embrace the environmental accountabilities necessary for conscientious bicycling; staffers in Local Motion on the other hand have tended to view people like Carl and Leslie as potential allies but ones already converted to the cause of active transportation and, anyway, too focused on their individual concerns. Whether or not they actually are part of the same cause is an open question.

Defining a common agenda for bicycle advocacy in Burlington has yet to really become a major issue, and few calls have been made for a unified front. Perhaps it is because of the recognizable difficulties involved in reconciling the range of positions, ideologies, and strategies for making change within Burlington's bike movement—of which I've only covered a few in this chapter—or perhaps based in the idea that there is a kind of strength-in-diversity. Indeed, as one staffer at Local Motion once observed to me, "All social movements are fragmented. It's a sign that more people are coming into the fold with new ideas." With the bicycle's recent rise in public profile, there is little doubt that at least the second point is accurate—more people *are* coming into the fold. But regarding the first point, what we might expect to see in coming years is intensifying discussions over what's good for the cause, if not what the cause itself actually is.

For Further Exploration

During the past few years, there has been a minor explosion in the number of useful and interesting books on bicycle advocacy and politics, though none of them are ethnographic or anthropological in orientation. These studies include political scientist Harry Wray's *Pedal Power: The Quiet Rise of the Bicycle in American Public Life* (http://www.paradigmpublishers.com/books/BookDetail.

aspx?productID=180326) and political journalist Jeff Mapes' *Pedaling Revolution: How Cyclists are Changing American Cities* (http://osupress.oregonstate.edu/book/pedaling-revolution), both of which describe well the legislation, elite decision-makers, and leaders of the U.S. bicycle movement; the second also has a good overview of the intersections between health policy and bicycling. Cultural Studies scholar Zack Furness' landmark study *One Less Car: Bicycling and the Politics of Automobility* is another important work, which situates bicycle politics as an expression of resistance to automobile domination and as a site of popular culture expression (http://www.temple.edu/tempress/titles/1899_reg.html).

For more background on Critical Mass and a list of rides see: http://criticalmass.wikia.com/wiki/List_of_rides. Chris Carlsson, a writer who has been involved in Critical Mass for a long time and other expressions of what he calls "outlaw cycling" has published several books of interest about the topic, *Critical Mass: Bicycling's Defiant Celebration* (http://www.akpress.org/criticalmassbicyclings defiantcelebration.html) and *Nowtopia: How Pirate Programmers, Outlaw Bicyclists, and Vacant-Lot Gardeners are Inventing the Future Today!* (http://www.processed world.com/carlsson/nowtopia_web/index.shtml).

The National Bike Summit has in recent years become an important venue for the bike movement, and since it is held in Washington, D.C., politicians have taken notice. For background and information on the event, see the website for it here: http://www.bikeleague.org/conferences/summit12/.

Along with the League of American Bicyclists (http://www.bikeleague.org), the lobbying group Bikes Belong (http://www.bikesbelong.org/) and the Alliance for Biking and Walking (http://www.peoplepoweredmovement.org/site/) have gained an important profile as leaders of the bike movement at the U.S. national level. Bikes Belong sponsors the "People For Bikes" initiative (http://www.peopleforbikes.org/), which is an online petition and resource center for bicycling politics and policy.

Bicycle advocacy groups often publish "Advocacy Toolkits" on their websites to give their members resources to "take action." Local Motion's can be found here: http://www.localmotion.org/advocacy/advocacytoolkit.

5

CONCLUSION:
ON THE NEED FOR THE BICYCLE

"The mounted cyclist is a different person."
　　　　　　　　—Paul Fournel, *Need for the Bike*, 2003: 132

Need for the Bike is a unique book of essays on bicycles and bicycling. In it the author, French writer and diplomat Paul Fournel, explores through short vignettes the idea that cycling is a practice of life involving the dynamic interplay of moral, physical, and intellectual dimensions (Stoekel 2003). For the cyclist, according to Fournel, the bicycle lies at the heart of everyday communication and connection with oneself and others, whether it is in daily use getting around a city or on long rides of friendly competition among comrades. Riding a bicycle is thus not simply a matter of pedaling and balancing, which are issues of technique, but its own universe of daily experience and desire, involving pain, delight, mystery, violence, camaraderie, and embodied memories. It is also a universe of relationships with material objects, including "roads with texture," articles of clothing that enable or constrict movement, and of course, bicycles. "The desire to have a beautiful bike is something shared by everyone," he observes (Fournel 2003: 32). But as much as it pleases, Fournel is quick to point out that the bicycle also imposes demands on its rider, shaping, conditioning, and challenging the body and psyche in specific ways.

Of the many ideas Fournel explores, one of the most suggestive is the idea quoted above, that the mounted cyclist is a different person than when he or she is not on a bicycle. Fournel makes this observation in the midst of a discussion about the relationship between eating and cycling, observing that while riding a bicycle his taste for certain foods changes, so that foods he likes to eat when he's not riding he can't stand while on the bike, and things he normally won't eat are highly appetizing during a ride. For Fournel, this oddity is a lesson in what he calls "the nonconcurrence of pleasures," and an opportunity to explore on a deeper level the role of the bicycle in mediating the intersections of hunger and satisfaction. The "need for the bike" here lies in its ability to reveal insights about the human condition that might not otherwise be apparent.

In important respects, Fournel's notion of bicycling as a practice of life aligns well with the approach taken in this book, which is that a critical understanding of mobilities recognizes that means of travel and transportation are not just empty vessels for moving through space but themselves entail the development and performance of distinctive skills, symbolic meanings, ideological positionings, and moral quandaries. Both of our approaches accept that the bicycle and bicycling are not straightforward or self-evident facts, but require some critical estrangement and digging around in that experience to be fully appreciated. But my own approach in this book is rooted in a different conceptualization of what it means to situate bicycling as a practice of life. While Fournel's approach is based in a deep and considered exploration of his own subjective experience with bicycles, my argument here has been based on an ethnographically informed perspective that practices of life—not to mention the need for the bicycle—are rooted in cultural, social, and political-economic processes, even as they involve important individual and subjective experiences.

From an anthropological point of view, then, to suggest that the mounted cyclist is a different person implies something quite distinct, but it too reveals meaningful insights, especially about conditions and dilemmas involved in everyday life, as well as the cultural processes, social changes, and power relations that help shape those conditions and dilemmas. For example, as explored in Chapter 2, symbolic meanings in the U.S. that cast bicycles as technologically static, primitive, and obsolete vis-à-vis automobiles can turn an otherwise serious adult who gets around by bicycle into someone who is categorically unadult, even childish. Similarly, as noted in Chapter 3, the common view in the U.S. that riding a bicycle in a city is stupid, crazy, or asking for trouble can change that same adult into a foolish maniac. In both of these cases, the mounted cyclist is symbolically transformed into someone who is abnormal or deviant, not to be taken seriously even if his or her intentions are quite serious. These transformations of status have concrete impacts in the world, reflecting and reinforcing a hierarchically arranged system of mobility in which the symbolic prestige, economic investment, and political support flow to the interests of motorized transportation.

Of course, one of the major points of this book has been that, although these meanings of bicycle mobility as abnormal may feel natural to some, they are not automatic or universal. They are the product of particular historical, cultural, and political-economic circumstances. There are important cross-cultural variations and unevenness in how people approach bicycles and the activity of getting around on a bicycle in everyday life, as well as variations that play out within societies across categories of gender, class, age, and ethnicity. Throughout their history, bicycles have been closely tied to dynamics of social differentiation, such as the association between bicycles and progressive modernity in the 1890s, or the association between bicycles and expressive politics of local-ism and sustainable lifestyles in recent decades. In individual cities and coun-tries, these dynamics of variation and differentiation, as discussed in Chapter 3, are closely related to factors such as the reconfiguration of urban spaces to handle increasing demands of urban mobility; infrastructure, policies, and pro-grams that are intended to support and encourage bicycle riding; individual preferences and embodied experiences associated with daily mobility; percep-tions of urban space; the social norms and informal codes related to the actual practice of riding a bicycle; and not least, attitudes toward the bicycle itself. It is important to recognize that these factors are as likely to shape actual conditions of bicycling in a city for some as they are to make it seem unimaginable for others.

The other major point here has been that symbolic meanings of bicycles are in flux, especially in urban areas where concerns over environmental sustaina-bility, public health, global competitiveness, car-choked streets, and the finan-cial limitations of current patterns of public spending are on the table as key leaders, decision-makers, and community activists struggle over the future of cities. Some of those shifts in meaning can be directly attributed to the effec-tiveness of bicycle advocates and their allies in transportation planning circles, environmentalism, and public health in framing how bicycles can legitimately address a range of contemporary problems. These claimants often emphasize, quite literally, the *need for the bike*, and rooted in a version of Fournel's point above, assert that the mounted cyclist is a different person: happier, healthier, and with a greener footprint on the world. One conviction that stems from this view is that bicycles can bring about large-scale social change and improve-ments in conditions of urban life when enough people experience the bicycle as a vehicle of personal transformation—and cities such as Amsterdam are held up as illustrations of that idea. Not all people aligned with the bicycle cause, of course, agree with that position. As expressed by one writer and advocate, "The bicycle won't solve the world's problems. That rocket has launched. It could very well solve some of yours, however. On an individual level, the bicycle trans-forms lives, in times of plenty and times of hardship" (Hurst 2009: 6). For still others, it is difficult to accept the need for the bicycle if all it does is aid the expansion of global commodity markets and doesn't address the unsustainabil-ity of contemporary consumption patterns. That these kinds of contradictory perspectives exist within the bike movement should come as no surprise, for, as I described in Chapter 4, it is an unfolding, flexible, and emergent arena of cultural politics in which basic categories, such as the meaning of the bicycle itself, remain unsettled as deeper differences of political philosophy, morality, and social identity play out.

Whatever one's attitude toward the need for the bicycle as a political or per-sonal issue, it is important to remember that needs are culturally constructed.

Even the most natural-seeming needs, such as eating or shelter, and—in the case of the themes this book treats—the need to get around in one's environment, are shaped by the shared preferences and imperatives of culture. With the bicycle, these processes of construction can be seen at multiple social levels: in the momentous decisions of political-economic actors and institutions that impact the shape and structure of an urban mobility system, thus creating the "need" people have to get around in certain ways; in the ways that bicycle peddlers construct the "need" to consume bicycles and their accessories through the careful production of imageries of desire in marketing and promotion; and in the rather mundane day-to-day decisions and activities of those people actually moving around on streets, pathways, and roads, who "need" to perform certain actions and develop certain skills to conduct their daily lives. That the construction of these needs does not take place on an equal playing field due to inequalities of wealth and power can generate social competition, struggle, and the exercise of social control. Needs are often artificially imposed and resisted, and it is interesting to consider how the bike movement has been making the case with increasing public success that the imposition of the "need" for automobiles has undermined urban environments and quality of life.

Throughout all these high-stakes processes, it is easy to let the actual object, the bicycle itself, fade into the background. Bicycles are rooted in a symbolic order in which people create particular cultural meanings and status hierarchies through the consumption and possession of material things. But while bicycles are always symbolic, they are not simply symbols. Their materiality—that is, their physical properties and temporal dimensions—contributes to the experience and perceptions of the user, as well as the social relations surrounding the object. And this is yet another reading on Fournel's observation about the mounted cyclist being a different person. Riding a bicycle constrains the body in certain ways and generates sensations as it extends a rider's locomotive capabilities and interacts with the ground. The experiential and physical specificities involved in bicycle riding are precisely the kind of focus that consumes a lot of attention among people who ride bicycles whether it is for pleasure, exercise, or utilitarian purposes, and the differences between riding a bicycle and walking or riding in a train, for example, should be apparent to anyone who has done each.

But it is important as well to recognize in all this that "the bicycle" is not a unitary or monolithic thing. It is a heterogeneous, multidimensional, and contextual object. Throughout their history, bicycles have taken on many distinct physical and technical forms, forms that have been put to use in pursuing diverse social, political, and technological agendas. That dynamism continues today as bicycle builders and manufacturers respond to and help shape people's perceptions of the diverse things one can do with a bicycle, including using it for practical, everyday mobility. What is important about these processes is that they are an important expression of the way ordinary things acquire social lives and in turn shape social relations in sometimes extraordinary ways. It seems fair to conclude that here is yet another dimension of the "need" for bicycles, which is to remind us of how complicated and deep are the ways humans interact with the objects they create.

NOTES

2 WHAT (AND WHEN) IS A BICYCLE?

1 Early cyclists often compared the bicycle to the train, another key technology of modernity. Due to its size and timetables, the train was viewed as swallowing people, forcing them to adapt their behavior to the train, while the bicycle endowed the individual with control (Ebert 2004).

2 In the introduction to the book *Objects and Others*, historian of anthropology George Stocking (1988) offers a very brief and schematic, but richly suggestive, framing of the multidimensionality of objects. My approach here is both inspired by Stocking's brief discussion and seeks to extend it.

3 CONSTRUCTING URBAN BICYCLE CULTURES: PERSPECTIVES ON THREE CITIES

1 The name Zach, like all names of people drawn from my ethnographic fieldwork in Burlington in this chapter and the next, is a pseudonym, which is an anthropological convention intended to protect the identity of an informant.

2 These dynamics of decentralization have played out differently in distinct places. A number of cities, among them Chicago and Los Angeles, decentralized around multiple centers connected by newly built expressways.

3 China, which was once known as "the Bicycle Kingdom," has a number of cities where bicycle usage is high, including Beijing, Shanghai, and numerous provincial cities such as Shijiazhuang, where in the year 2000, 56 percent of trips taken by the city's 2.14 million people were by bicycle (Ma, Cao, and Fan 2007; Haixiao 2012). The main reason the government promoted cycling as a form of mass transportation had to do with the low cost of producing bicycles and the low infrastructure costs (Mohagadass 2003).

4 One study observes that in Beijing, this speed and efficiency extends to the bicycle as a useful alternative to public transit as well. Within six kilometers, bicycles are faster than buses and subways, and remain competitive up to ten kilometers (Gardner 1998).

5 "New Urbanism" is an urban design movement that emphasizes walkable and bicycle-friendly neighborhoods, as well as mixed residential and commercial development. The Charter of the New Urbanism, an important text in the movement states:

> "We advocate the restructuring of public policy and development practices to support the following principles: neighborhoods should be diverse in use and population; communities should be designed for the pedestrian and transit as well as the car; cities and towns should be shaped by physically defined and universally accessible public spaces and community institutions; urban places should be framed by architecture and landscape design that celebrate local history, climate, ecology, and building practice."
>
> (http://www.cnu.org/charter)

6 The Dutch situation differs radically from other bicycle-obsessed European countries, such as France and Italy, whose national identities became closely associated with bicycle racing. Even while common, the status of everyday cycling in these countries has never had the social legitimacy and prestige of racing.

7 In 1923, for example, 74 percent of traffic on state roads in the Netherlands was bicycles; 11 percent were motorcars, and 5 percent were motorcycles. The close identification between the Dutch and bicycles endured through World War II when the Nazis appropriated 50,000 bicycles from the Netherland for their war effort, causing national outrage (Carstensen and Ebert 2012).

8 Here I should explain the origins of my following attempt to characterize the conventions and practices involved in cycling in Amsterdam. I have not actually been to Amsterdam, which could be construed as a black mark within a discipline that places a strong emphasis on "being there" as a way of generating knowledge. Yet every anthropologist relies on the work of other scholars to help generate their own insights—which I am doing here as well by combining insights from Pelzer (2010), Carstensen and Ebert (2012), and Kuipers (2012). Further, I've become a keen viewer of YouTube, where videos about cycling in Amsterdam proliferate and in which locals often share their attitudes and experiences of cycling. See the YouTube channel "Cycling in the Netherlands" (http://www.youtube.com/user/markenlei). In addition, I've followed and analyzed various blogs that report (in English) on the daily practice of bicycle mobility in Amsterdam and other cities in the Netherlands, including Bicycle Dutch (http://bicycledutch.wordpress.com/); Amsterdamize (www.amsterdamize.com); Bakfiets en Meer (http://www.workcycles.com/blog); and A View from the Cycle Path (www.aviewfromthecyclepath.com). I am intensely aware of the limitations of these data sources, but my goal here is to *characterize*, not represent, the experience of riding Amsterdam's streets.

9 This notion of thinking of bicycles as appliances should be credited to Mikael Colville-Andersen, a well-known blogger who writes about cycling in Copenhagen (www.copenhagenize.com).

10 A similar issue is reported by Pelzer, who quotes a young student: "When there are like a lot of traffic lights for small streets I'll just pass them and sometimes I'll ride on the sidewalk . . . Are there traffic regulations! . . . You know, at the dangerous spots you have to stop, but usually, when they can go, they go" (Pelzer 2010: 5).

11 Montes et al. 2011 report that in a 2005 survey, 46.2 percent of the total adult users were bicyclists, 47.9 percent were pedestrians, and 5.9 percent engaged in other activities.

12 *Ciclovía* has overwhelming popular support and in 2000 residents approved other car-free initiatives, including an annual car-free day during a weekday (Ardila and Menckhoff 2004). As Ardila and Menckhoff report, the administration held a referendum in October 2000. Citizens were asked whether the city should establish a car-free day on the first Thursday of every February, and whether to ban all cars from circulating during two 3-hour peak periods per day, starting in 2015. A large majority approved the first, and this car-free day has been held since 2001. A slim majority approved the second proposal. Business leaders, led by the National Federation of Retailers, took the city to court, which ruled that the total number of people who voted in this question (either yes, no, or blank vote) was not above the constitutional minimum for making the referendum valid. So the second was rejected.

13 There are currently three platinum cities in the BFC program, Portland, Oregon, Davis, California, and Boulder, Colorado. In these cities, rates of bicycle mode share are among the highest in the U.S. In Portland, for example, upwards of 6 percent of commuting trips are made by bicycle.

14 Here are some of the key details about Burlington. In terms of Engineering, it has infrastructure on more than 10 percent of its roads to accommodate cyclists—most of it is bike lane markings and paved shoulders, but there is also a buffered bike lane, one contra-flow lane, paved shoulders, various road diet projects, and shared-lane markings ("sharrows"). City planning officials are also well-versed in techniques to accommodate

bicyclists, and the city just passed a "Complete Streets" resolution. Regarding Education and Encouragement, numerous initiatives in the city exist to inform and inspire cyclists, from public media campaigns to raise awareness about bicycle safety and bike skills courses for kids to cyclist-specific financial incentive programs, fun rides, and various bicycle clubs for local cyclists. In the area of Enforcement, police officers are trained in cycling law, and local ordinances protect cyclists, such as a law that requires motorists to give cyclists three feet of space when passing them, as well bans on texting while driving. Concerning Evaluation and Planning, the city has a bicycle master plan that orients and prioritizes transportation planning decisions.

15 These plans include a climate action plan to reduce greenhouse gas emissions, an updated city transportation plan, the city's land use plan, and various documents envisioning a green, healthy, and sustainable future city.

4 "GOOD FOR THE CAUSE": THE BIKE
MOVEMENT AS SOCIAL ACTION AND CULTURAL POLITICS

1 It is perhaps worthwhile to note here that urban socialists in the U.S. were divided on the bicycle. Even with the bicycle's reputation for promoting equality, Furness (2010) observes that some socialists in the 1890s fought bicycle traffic and plans to pave certain streets, which would lead to greater bicycle traffic through certain urban neighborhoods.

2 One of the notable exceptions to this weak situation regarding funding mechanisms is the "Oregon Bicycle Bill" passed by the Oregon state legislature in 1971. It required the state Department of Transportation to provide facilities for bicycles and pedestrians when building road infrastructure, and mandated at least 1 percent of state funds from the federal government be used for bicycle and pedestrian infrastructure.

3 The outlines of the story are this: The city had slated a $^3/_4$ mile-long stretch of an important traffic corridor for repaving. By declaring it a Complete Streets demonstration project, the idea was that after repaving, a different configuration of lines would be painted on the asphalt, reducing the road from four lanes intended for cars only, to two car lanes, a center turn lane, and bike lanes on each side—thus meeting the spirit of Complete Streets by taking all users into account in road projects. Before repaving, the Department of Public Works, painted down temporary lines with the new configuration and sought public feedback. As the period for feedback seemed to be extending months beyond what was expected, the Department announced that it was having trouble getting feedback from automobile commuters who live outside the city and so needed more time. Meanwhile, rumors began circulating that a powerful city councilor and several members of the Public Works Commission were against the new configuration and that fear of offending them was holding up the project. Whether or not it is actually true is somewhat irrelevant here; the major issue is that it was during this time that Local Motion mounted its quiet campaign to inundate Public Works with complementary letters to follow through with the new configuration.

BIBLIOGRAPHY

Adams, J. 2001. *Hypermobility: Too Much of a Good Thing.* London: PIU Transport Seminar.

Alliance for Biking & Walking. 2012. "Bicycling and Walking in the United States. 2012 Benchmarking Report." Washington, D.C.: Alliance for Biking & Walking.

Alvarez, Sonia, E. Dagnino and Arturo Escobar. 1998. "Introduction: The Cultural and Political in Latin American Social Movements." In *Cultures of Politics/Politics of Cultures: Re-Visioning Latin American Social Movements,* edited by Sonia Alvarez, E. Dagnino, and Arturo Escobar, 1–29. Boulder: Westview Press.

Amit, Vered. 2000. "Introduction: Constructing the Field" In Vered Amit, ed. *Constructing the Field: Ethnographic Fieldwork in the Contemporary World.* London: Routledge, pp. 1–18.

Amsterdamize. 2011. "Unfazed and Nonplussed." World Wide Website accessed on Jul 12, 2012: http://amsterdamize.com/2011/11/22/unfazed-and-nonplussed/.

Appadurai, Arjun, ed. 1986. *The Social Life of Things: Commodities in Cultural Perspective.* Cambridge: Cambridge University Press.

—1996. *Modernity at Large: Cultural Dimensions of Globalization.* Minneapolis: University of Minnesota Press.

Ardila, Arturo and Gerhard Menckhoff. 2002. "Transportation Policies in Bogota, Colombia: Building a Transportation System for the People." *Transportation Research Record* 181: 130–136.

Aronson, Sidney. 1952. "The Sociology of the Bicycle." *Social Forces* 30(3): 305–312.

Augé, Marc. 2002. *In the Metro.* Minneapolis: University of Minnesota Press.

Bae, Chang-Hee Christine. 2004. "Transportation and the Environment." In *The Geography of Urban Transportation,* edited by Susan Hanson and Genevieve Guiliano, 356–381. New York: Guilford Press.

Batterbury, Simon. 2003. "Environmental Activism and Social Networks: Campaigning for Bicycles and Alternative Transport in West London." *The ANNALS of the American Academy of Political and Social Science* 2003 590: 150–169.

Bauman, Zygmunt. 2000. *Liquid Modernity.* Cambridge: Polity.

Beckett, Katherine and Angelina Godoy. 2010. "A Tale of Two Cities: A Comparative Analysis of Quality of Life Initiatives in New York and Bogotá." *Urban Studies Journal* 47(2): 277–301, February 2010.

Berney, Rachel. 2010. "Learning from Bogotá: How Municipal Experts Transformed Public Space." *Journal of Urban Design* 15(4): 539–558, November 2010.

Bicycle Retailer. 2011. "2011 Sales Training Guide." PDF accessed on May 17, 2012: http://www.bicycleretailer.com/resources/resourceDetail/420.html.

Bjiker, Wiebe. 1995. *Of Bicycles, Bakelites, and Bulbs: Toward a Theory of Sociotechnical Change.* Cambridge, MA: MIT Press.

Blickstein, Susan. 2010. "Automobility and the Politics of Bicycling in New York City." *International Journal of Urban and Regional Research* 34(4): 886–905.

Blue, Elly. 2010. "There's Safety in Numbers for Cyclists." *Grist.* World Wide Website accessed on July 20, 2012: http://grist.org/article/2010-10-11-theres-safety-in-numbers-for-cyclists/

Bourdieu, Pierre. 1979. *Distinction: A Social Critique of the Judgement of Taste.* New York: Routledge.

Brightspoke. 2011. "Understanding Bike Frame Materials." World Wide Website accessed on May 17, 2012: http://www.brightspoke.com/c/understanding/bike-frame-materials. html.

Brown, Lester. 2010. "The Welcome Return of the Bicycle." World Wide Website accessed on May 17, 2012: http://www.treehugger.com/cars/the-welcome-return-of-the-bicycle.html.

Brown, Sheldon. n.d. "A Revisionist Theory of Bicycle Sizing." World Wide Web site accessed on June 29, 2012: http://www.sheldonbrown.com/frame-sizing.html

Brussel, Mark and Mark Zuidgeest. 2012. "Cycling in Developing Countries: Context, Challenges, and Policy Relevant Research." In *Cycling and Sustainability*, edited by John Parkin, 181–216. Bingley, UK: Emerald Publishing Group.

Buehler, Ralph and John Pucher. 2010. "Cycling to Sustainability in Amsterdam." *Sustain* 21. Fall/Winter 2010: 36–40

Buendía, Felipe Cala. 2010. "More Carrots than Sticks: Antanas Mockus's Civic Culture Policy in Bogotá." *New Directions for Youth Development* 125: 19–32.

Caldeira, Teresa. 1999. "Fortified Enclaves: The New Urban Segregation." In *Theorizing the City: The New Urban Anthropology Reader*, edited by Setha Low, 83–110. New Brunswick, NJ: Rutgers University Press

Carlsson, Chris, ed. 2002. *Critical Mass: Cycling's Defiant Celebration.* Oakland, CA: AK Press.

Carrier, James. 2004. "Consumption and Anthropology: Limits to Culture?" Paper presented at Knowing Consumers: Actors, Images, Identities in Modern History. Conference at the Zentrum für Interdisziplinäre Forschung in Bielefeld, Germany. February 26–28, 2004.

Carstensen, Trine Agervig and Anne-Katrin Ebert. 2012. "Cycling Cultures in Northern Europe: From 'Golden Age' to 'Renaissance.'" In *Cycling and Sustainability*, edited by John Parkin, 23–58. Bingley, UK: Emerald Publishing Group.

Cass, Noel, Elizabeth Shove and John Urry. 2005. "Social Exclusion, Mobility, and Access." *The Sociological Review* 53: 539–555.

CCB (Cámara de Comercio de Bogotá). 2009. *Movilidad en Bicicleta en Bogotá.* World Wide Web site accessed on 6/25/12: http://www.ccb.org.co.

Cervero, Robert, Olga L. Sarmiento, Enrique Jacoby, Luis Fernando Gomez, and Andrea Neiman. 2009. "Influences of Built Environments on Walking and Cycling: Lessons from Bogota." *International Journal of Sustainable Transportation* 3: 203–226.

City of Chicago. 2005. "Bike 2015 Plan." World Wide Website accessed on 7/12/12: http://bike2015plan.org/intro.html

Clifford, James. 1997. *Routes: Travel and Translation in the Late Twentieth Century.* Cambridge, MA: Harvard University Press.

Comaroff, John. 2010. "The End of Anthropology, Again: On the Future of an In/Discipline." *American Anthropologist* 112(4): 524–538.

Cox, Peter. 2006. "Conflicting Agendas in Selling Cycling." Paper presented at Velo-City 2005, Dublin. Electronic version accessed June 12, 2010: http://chester.academia.edu/PeterCox/Papers/212490/Conflicting_Agendas_in_Selling_Cycling

—2008. "The Role of Human Powered Vehicles in Sustainable Mobility." *Built Environment* 34(2): 140–160.

Cox, Peter and Frederick Van De Walle. 2007. "Bicycles Don't Evolve: Velomobiles and the Modelling of Transport." In *Cycling and Society*, Horton, et al., 113–131. Burlington, VT: Ashgate Publishing.

Creswell, Tim. 2001. "The Production of Mobilities." *New Formations* 43: 11–25.

—2006. *On the Move: Mobility in the Modern Western World.* London: Routledge.

Dalsgaard, Andreas Møl. 2009. *Cities on Speed: Bogotá Change.* Copenhagen, DK: DR International.

Dávila Valencia, Mónica. 2010. "Etnografía de la Ciudad desde Bicicleta." In *La Investigación en Ciencias Sociales: Estrategias de Investigación*, edited by Pablo Páramo. Bogotá: Universidad Piloto.

Davis, Paul. 2011. "Are Bike Lanes Expressways to Gentrification?" Shareable: Cities. 8/30/11: http://www.shareable.net/blog/are-bike-lanes-an-expressway-to-gentrification

Deka, Devajyoti. 2004. "Social and Environmental Justice Issues in Urban Transportation." In *The Geography of Urban Transportation*, edited by Susan Hanson and Genevieve Guiliano, 332–355. New York: Guilford Press.

DeSena, Judith. 2009. *Gentrification and Inequality in Brooklyn: The New Kids on the Block*. Lanham, MD: Lexington Books.

di Leonardo, Micaela. 1998. *Exotics at Home: Anthropologies, Others, American Modernity*. Chicago: University of Chicago Press.

Douglas, Mary and Baron Isherwood. 1979. *The World of Goods*. New York: Basic Books.

Ebert, Anne-Katrin. 2004. "Cycling Towards the Nation: The Use of the Bicycle in Germany and the Netherlands, 1880–1940." *European Review of History* 11(3): 347–364.

Edwards, Ben. 2011. "Made in America." *Peloton Magazine*. October 2011: 50–53.

Ehn, Billy and Orvar Löfgren. 2010. *The Secret World of Doing Nothing*. Berkeley, CA: University of California Press.

Emanuel, Rahm. 2012. "City of Chicago Department of Transportation Bicycle Program." World Wide Website accessed on 7/12/12: http://chicagobikes.org/.

Epperson, Bruce D. 2010. *Peddling Bicycles to America: The Rise of an Industry*. Jefferson, NC: McFarland.

Federal Highway Administration. 2011. "Congestion: A National Issue." World Wide Website accessed on May 17, 2012: http://www.ops.fhwa.dot.gov/aboutus/opstory.htm

Fietsberaad (Dutch Cycling Council). 2006. "Continuous and Integral: The Cycling Policies of Groningen and other European Cycling Cities." World Wide Website accessed on July 12, 2012: http://www.fietsberaad.nl/index.cfm?lang=en&repository=Fietsberaad+publication+7.+Continuous+and+integral:+The+cycling+policies+of+Groningen+and+other+European+cycling+cities

—2010. "The Bicycle Capitals of the World: Amsterdam and Copenhagen." World Wide Website accessed on July 12, 2012: http://www.fietsberaad.nl/index.cfm?lang=en&repository=Fietsberaad+publication+7A+The+bicycle+capitals+of+the+world+Amsterdam+and+Copenhagen

Forbes, Jeff McMahon. 2012. "Cities Expect Bicycle Boom." *Chicago Tribune*. July 12, 2012. http://www.chicagotribune.com/news/plus/nsc-cities-expect-bicycle-boom-20120712,0,7781640.story?dssReturn

Forester, John. 1977/2008. "Effective Cycling Instructor's Manual." Sixth edition. World Wide Web site accessed on 27 September 2010: www.johnforester.com/BTEO/ECIM6.pdf

Formosa, Nicole. 2011. "Retail Recovery: Specialty Sales Rebound from Recession Lows." *Bicycle Retailer and Industry News* 20(11): 1, 28.

Fournel, Paul. 2003. *Need for the Bike*. Translated by Allan Stoekel. Lincoln, NE: University of Nebraska Press.

Fowler, Cynthia. 2011. "Performing Pisgah: Endurance Mountain Bikers Generating the National Forest." *Anthropology News* 53(2): 11.

Fox, Richard and Orin Starn. 1997. *Between Resistance and Revolution: Cultural Politics and Social Protest*. New Brunswick, NJ: Rutgers University Press.

Freudendahl-Pedersen, Malene. 2009. *Mobility in Daily Life: Between Freedom and Unfreedom*. Burlington, VT: Ashgate Publishing.

Freund, Peter and George Martin. 2007. "Hypermobility: The Social Organization of Space, and Health." *Mobilities* 2: 37–49.

Fricker, Alan. 1998. "Measuring Up to Sustainability." *Futures* 30(4): 367–375.

Furness, Zach. 2010. *One Less Car: Bicycling and the Politics of Automobility*. Philadelphia: Temple University Press.

Gardner, Gary. 1998. "When Cities Take Bicycles Seriously." *World Watch* Sep/Oct 1998 11(5): 16–23.

Garvey, Ellen. 1996. *The Adman in the Parlor: Magazines and the Gendering of Consumer Culture, 1880s to 1910s.* New York: Oxford University Press.

Gilley, Brian. 2006. "Cyclist Subjectivity: Corporeal Management and the Inscription of Suffering." *Anthropological Notebooks* 12(2): 53–64.

Goodman, J. David. 2010. "Expansion of Bike Lanes in City Brings Backlash." *New York Times,* November 22, 2010: http://www.nytimes.com/2010/11/23/nyregion/23bicycle.html

Grafton-Small, Robert. 1987. "Marketing, or the Anthropology of Consumption." *European Journal of Marketing* 21(9): 66–71.

Grant, Christine. 2012. "Why We Fall in Love with Cycling." World Wide Website accessed on May 2, 2012: http://daily.sightline.org/2012/05/02/why-we-fall-in-love-with-cycling/?utm_source=Sightline+Newsletters&utm_campaign=63e73c7004-SightlineWeekly&utm_medium=email.

Gupta, Akhil and James Ferguson. 1997. *Culture, Power, and Place: Explorations in Critical Anthropology.* Durham, NC: Duke University Press.

Hagen, Jonas. 2003. "Of Bicycles and Bipeds in Bogotá." *UN Chronicle* (2003) 2: 76–77.

Haixiao, Pan. 2012. "Evolution of Bicycle Transport Policy in China." In *Cycling and Sustainability,* edited by John Parkin, 161–180. Bingley, UK: Emerald Publishing Group.

Hall, Tim. 2003. "*Car*-ceral Cities: Social Geographies of Everyday Urban Mobility." In *Urban Futures: Critical Commentaries on Shaping the City,* edited by Malcolm Miles and Tim Hall, 92–105. London: Routledge.

Hanlon, Bernadette, John Short, and Thomas Vicino. 2010. *Cities and Suburbs: New Metropolitan Realities in the U.S.* New York: Routledge.

Hart, Tom. 2001. "Transport and the City." In *Handbook of Urban Studies,* edited by Ronan Paddison, 102–123. London: Sage Publications.

Henbrow, David. 2009. "Anatomy of a reliable, everyday bicycle." A View from the Cycle Path . . . blog. Accessed on July 12, 2012: http://www.aviewfromthecyclepath.com/2009/01/anatomy-of-reliable-everyday-bicycle.html

Herlihy, David. 2004. *Bicycle: The History.* New Haven, CT: Yale University Press.

Hirsch, Eric. 2010. "Property and Persons: New Forms and Contests in the Era of Neoliberalism." *Annual Review of Anthropology* 2010, 39: 347–360.

Horton, Dave. 2006. "Environmentalism and the Bicycle." *Environmental Politics* 15(1):41–58.

—n.d. "Social Movements and the Bicycle." World Wide Website accessed on May 20, 2012: http://thinkingaboutcycling.wordpress.com/social-movements-and-the-bicycle/

Horton, Dave, Peter Cox, and Paul Rosen, eds. 2007. *Cycling and Society.* Burlington, VT: Ashgate Publishing.

Hurst, Robert. 2006. *The Art of Cycling: A Guide to Bicycling in 21st Century America.* 2nd edn. Helena, MT: Falcon Guides.

—2009. *The Cyclist's Manifesto: The Case for Riding on Two Wheels Instead of Four.* Helena, MT: Falcon Guides.

IDRD (Instiduto Distrital de Recreación y Deporte). n.d. "Historia de la CicloVía y RecreoVía." World Wide Website accessed on June 29, 2012: http://www.inbogota.com/transporte/ciclovia/historia.htm

IDU (Instituto de Desarollo Urbano). 2011. "Informe Red de Ciclorutas." Report prepared by the Instituto de Desarollo Urbano, Subdirección General de Desarollo Urbano, Dirección Ténica de Proyectos, Bogotá, Colombia.

Illich, Ivan. 1973. *Tools for Conviviality.* New York: Marion Boyers.

—1977. "Energy and Equity." In *Toward a History of Needs,* 110–143. New York: Pantheon Books.

Ingold, Timothy. 2004. "Culture on the Ground: The World Perceived Through the Feet." *Journal of Material Culture* 9: 315–340.

—2011. *Being Alive: Essays on Movement, Knowledge, and Description.* New York: Routledge.

Jacobs, Jane. 1992. *The Life and Death of Great American Cities.* New York: Vintage.

Jarvis, Helen, Andy C. Pratt, and Peter Cheng-Chong Wu. 2001. *The Secret Life of Cities: The Social Reproduction of Everyday Life.* Harlow: Prentice Hall.

Jensen, Ole B. 2009. "Foreword: Mobilities as Culture." In *Cultures of Alternative Mobilities: Routes Less Traveled*, edited by Philip Vannini, xv–xix. Burlington, VT: Ashgate Publishing.

Jirón, Paola. 2009. "Immobile Mobility in Daily Travel Experiences in Santiago de Chile." In *Cultures of Alternative Mobilities: Routes Less Traveled*, edited by Philip Vannini, 127–140 Burlington, VT: Ashgate Publishing.

Jones, David E.H. 1970. "The Stability of the Bicycle." *Physics Today* 23(4): 34–40.

Jones, David. 2008. *Mass Motorization + Mass Transit: An American History and Policy Analysis*. Bloomington, IN: Indiana University Press.

Kopytoff, Igor. 1986. "The Cultural Biography of Things: Commoditization as Process." In *The Social Life of Things: Commodities in Cultural Perspective*, edited by Arjun Appadurai, 64–91. Cambridge: Cambridge University Press.

Krizek, Kevin J. 2012. "Cycling, Urban Form and Cities: What Do We Know and How Should We Respond?" In *Cycling and Sustainability*, edited by John Parkin, 111–130. Bingley, UK: Emerald Publishing Group.

Kuipers, Giselinde. 2012. "The Rise and Decline of National Habitus: Dutch Cycling Culture and the Shaping of National Similarity." *European Journal of Social Theory* 12(2): 1–19.

LaHood, Ray. 2010. "My view from atop the table at the National Bike Summit." World Wide Website accessed on May 17, 2012: http://fastlane.dot.gov/2010/03/my-view-from-atop-the-table-at-the-national-bike-summit.html

Lawrence, Denise, and Setha Low. 1990. "The Built Environment and Spatial Form." *Annual Reviews of Anthropology* 19: 453–505.

League of American Bicyclists. 2012. List of Bicycle Friendly Communities. World Wide Web site accessed on June 27, 2012: http://www.bikeleague.org/programs/bicyclefriendlyamerica/communities/

Lee, Brian. 2011. "International Approaches to Bicycle Planning." Bicycle Master Planning course, University of Vermont, March 21, 2011.

Lepeska, David. 2011. "City Bike Plan is Accused of Neighborhood Bias." *New York Times*, October 15, 2011. http://www.nytimes.com/2011/10/16/us/chicago-bike-plan-accused-of-neighborhood-bias.html

Litman, Todd. 2003. "Reinventing Transportation: Exploring the Paradigm Shift Needed to Reconcile Transportation and Sustainability Objectives." Victoria Transport Policy Institute, British Columbia, Canada.

—2011. "Generated Traffic and Induced Travel: Implications for Transport Planning." Victoria Transport Policy Institute, British Columbia, Canada.

—2012. "Whose Roads? Evaluating Bicyclists' and Pedestrians' Rights to Use Public Roadways." Victoria Transport Policy Institute, British Columbia, Canada.

Low, Setha, ed. 1999. *Theorizing the City: The New Urban Anthropology Reader*. New Brunswick, NJ: Rutgers University Press.

Lutz, Catherine and Anne Lutz Fernandez. 2010. *Carjacked: The Culture of the Automobile & its Effects on Our Lives*. New York: Palgrave Macmillan.

Mackintosh, Philip Gordon, and Glen Norcliffe. 2007 "Men, Women, and the Bicycle: Gender and Social Geography of Cycling in the Late Nineteenth Century." In *Cycling and Society*, edited by Dave Horton, Peter Cox, and Paul Rosen, 153–178. Burlington, VT: Ashgate Publishing.

Macy, Sue. 2011. *Wheels of Change: How Women Rode the Bicycle to Freedom*. Washington, D.C.: National Geographic.

Mapes, Jeff. 2009. *Pedaling Revolution: How Cyclists are Changing American Cities*. Corvallis, OR: Oregon State Press.

Martin, G. and M. Ceballos 2004. *Bogotá: Anatomía de una Transformación, Políticas de Seguridad Ciudadana 1995–2003*. Bogotá, Colombia: Editorial Pontificia Universidad Javeriana.

Marx, Karl. 1867/1976. *Capital: A Critique of Political Economy. Vol. 1*. Translated by Ben Fowkes. New York: Penguin Classics.

Massey, Doreen. 1993. "Power Geometry and a Progressive Sense of Place." In *Mapping the Futures: Local Cultures, Global Change*, edited by John Bird et al., 59–69. London: Routledge.

McCracken, Grant. 1988. *Culture & Consumption*. Bloomington, IN: Indiana University Press.

Mike's Bogotá Bike Blog. 2011. "Bicycle Theft on La Ciclovía—Redux!" World Wide Website accesssed on June 20, 2012: http://mikesbogotabikeblog.blogspot.com/2011/02/bicycle-theft-on-la-ciclovia-redux.html

—2012. "The Return of the 26th Street Ciclovía." World Wide Website accessed on June 20, 2012: http://mikesbogotabikeblog.blogspot.com/2012/08/the-return-of-26th-street-ciclovia.html.

Miller, Daniel. 1987. *Material Culture and Mass Consumption*. Oxford: Basil Blackwell.

—1998a. *A Theory of Shopping*. Ithaca, NY: Cornell University Press.

—2001. *The Dialectics of Shopping*. Chicago: University of Chicago Press.

—2010. *Stuff*. Malden, MA: Polity.

Miller, Daniel, ed. 1998b. *Material Cultures: Why Some Things Matter*. Chicago: University of Chicago Press.

Moghaddass, Amir. 2003. "The Bicycle's Long Way to China. The Appropriation of Cycling as a Foreign Cultural Technique 1860–1940." *Cycle History 13: Proceedings from the 13th International Cycling History Conference*, Ch. 14.

Montes, Felipe, et al. 2011. "Do Health Benefits Outweigh the Costs of Mass Recreational Programs? An Economic Analysis of Four Ciclovía Programs." *Journal of Urban Health: Bulletin of the New York Academy of Medicine* 89(1): 153–170.

Montezuma, Ricardo. 2005. "The Transformation of Bogotá, Colombia, 1995–2000. Investing in Citizenship and Urban Mobility." *Global Urban Development* 1(1): 1–10.

—2006. "Promoción de Modos de Vida Activos y Espacios Urbanos Saludables: La Transformación Cultural y Espacial de Bogotá Colombia" In *Nutrición y Vida Activa. Del Conocimiento a la Acción*, edited by W. Freire. Bogotá, Colombia: OPS Publicación Científica y Técnica No 612.

—2008. *La Ciudad del Tranvía: 1880–1920. Bogotá: Transformaciones Urbanas y Movilidad*. Bogotá: Editorial Universidad del Rosario.

Nash, June. 2004. "Introduction: Social Movements and Global Processes." In *Social Movements: An Anthropological Reader*, edited by June Nash, 1–26. Malden, MA: Wiley-Blackwell.

National Bicycle Dealers Association. 2010. "A Look at the Bicycle Industry's Vital Statistics." World Wide Website accessed on May 17, 2012: http://nbda.com/articles/industry-overview-2010-pg34.htm.

National Household Travel Survey. PDF accessed on May 17, 2012: http://nhts.ornl.gov/publications.shtml

Norcliffe, Glen. 1997. "Popeism and Fordism: Examining the Roots of Mass Production." *Regional Studies* 31(3): 267–80.

—2007. "On the Technical and Social Significance of the Tricycle." In *Cycle History 17: Proceedings of the Seventeenth International Cycling History Conference*, 59–68.

Nwabughuogu, Anthony. 1984. "The Role of Bicycle Transport in the Economic Development of Eastern Nigeria." *Journal of Transport History* 5(1): 91–98.

Ober, Lauren. 2010. "When it Comes to Bike Safety, Vermont Falls Down—Hard." *Seven Days*, 6/16/10. World Wide Web site accessed on June 27, 2012: http://www.7dvt.com/2010when-it-comes-bike-safety-vermont-falls-down-hard

O'Rourke, P.J. 2011. "Dear Urban Cyclists: Go Play in Traffic." *Wall Street Journal*. April 2, 2011: http://online.wsj.com/article/SB10001424052748704050204576218600999993800.html?mod=wsj_share_twitter

Panday, Amit. 2009. "The Business of Bicycles." DARE. World Wide Website Accessed on May 17, 2012: http://dare.co.in/opportunities/manufacturing/the-business-of-bicycles.htm

Pardo, Carlos Felipe. 2010. "Transport Policy in Bogotá Ten Years after the 'Golden Age:' The Challenge of Being an Example." Presentation to GTZ (German Organization for Technical Cooperation), Stuttgart.

Parkin, John, ed. 2012. *Cycling and Sustainability*. Bingley, UK: Emerald Publishing Group.

Patton, Jason. 2005. "Multiple Worlds on Oakland's Streets: Social Practice and the Built Environment." *Visual Anthropology Review* 20(2): 36–56.

Pellow, Deborah. 1999. "The Power of Space in the Evolution of an Accra *Zongo.*" In *Theorizing the City: The New Urban Anthropology Reader,* edited by Setha Low, 277–316. New Brunswick, NJ: Rutgers University Press.

Pels, Dick, Kevin Hetherington, and Frédéric Vandenberghe. 2002. "The Status of the Object: Performances, Mediations, and Techniques." *Theory, Culture, and Society* 19(5/6): 1–21.

Pelzer, Peter. 2010. "Bicycling as a Way of Life: A Comparative Case Study of Portland, OR and Amsterdam." Paper presented at the 7th Cycling and Society Symposium, Oxford, England.

Peñalosa, Enrique. 2002. "Urban Transport and Urban Development: A Different Model." Berkeley: University of California, Center for Latin American Studies.

Penn, Robert. 2011. *It's All About the Bike: The Pursuit of Happiness on Two Wheels.* New York: Bloomsbury USA.

Petty, Ross. 1995. "Peddling the Bicycle in the 1890s: Mass Marketing Shifts into High Gear." *Journal of Macromarketing* 15: 32–46.

Pivato, Stephano. 1990. "The Bicycle as a Political Symbol: Italy, 1885–1955." *International Journal of the History of Sport* 7(2): 172–187.

Pridmore, Jay and Jim Hurd. 1995. *The American Bicycle.* Osceola, WI: Motorbooks International.

Pucher, John, Jennifer Dill, and Susan Handy. 2010. "Infrastructure, Programs, and Policies to Increase Bicycling: An International Review." *Preventive Medicine* 50: S106–S125.

Pucher, John and Ralph Buehler. 2008. "Making Cycling Irresistible: Lessons from the Netherlands, Denmark, and Germany." *Transport Reviews* 28(4): 495–528.

—2009 "Cycling for a Few or for Everyone: The Importance of Social Justice in Cycling Policy." *World Transport Policy & Practice* 15(1): 57–64.

Pucher, John and Lewis Dikstra. 2003. "Promoting Safe Walking and Cycling to Improve Public Health: Lessons from the Netherlands and Germany." *American Journal of Public Health* 93(9).

Pucher, John, Ralph Buehler, and Mark Seinen. 2011. "Bicycling Renaissance in North America? An Update and Reappraisal of Cycling Trends and Policies." *Transportation Research Part A* 45 (2011): 451–475.

Reitveld, Piet and Vanessa Daniel. 2004. "Determinants of Bicycle Use: Do Municipal Policies Matter?" *Transportation Research Part A* 38 (2004): 531-550.

Rendell, Matt. 2003. *Kings of the Mountains: How Colombia's Cycling Heroes Changed their Country's History.* London: Aurum Press.

Roberts, Kerry. 2008. "Where Was My Bike Made?" World Wide Website Accessed on May 17, 2012: http://thebikestand.com/who-made-my-bike.html

Robson, Anthony. 2012. "Anthsterdam." City Cyling blog. World Wide Website accessed on July 12, 2012: http://www.citycycling.co.uk/Issue2/Anthsterdam1.html

Rosen, Paul. 2002. *Framing Production: Technology, Culture, and Change in the British Bicycle Industry.* Cambridge, MA: MIT Press.

Rutheiser, Charles. 1999. "Making Place in the Nonplace Urban Realm: Notes on the Revitalization of Urban Atlanta." In *Theorizing the City: The New Urban Anthropology Reader,* edited by Setha Low, 317–341. New Brunswick, NJ: Rutgers University Press.

Ryan, John C. and Alan Thien Durning. 1997. *Stuff: The Secret Lives of Everyday Things.* Seattle: Northwest Environment Watch.

Sachs, Wolfgang. 1992. *For the Love of the Automobile: Looking Back into the History of our Desires.* Berkeley, CA: University of California Press.

Sapir, Edward. 1921. *Language: An Introduction to the Study of Speech.* New York: Harcourt, Brace.

Sarmiento, Olga, et al. 2010. "The Ciclovía-Recreativa: A Mass-Recreational Program With Public Health Potential." *Journal of Physical Activity and Health* 2010, 7(Suppl 2): S163–S180.

Schafer, Andreas and David Victor. 2000. "The Future Mobility of the World Population." *Transportation Research Part A* 34: 171–205.

Schwanen, Tim, Martin Dijst, and Frans M. Dieleman. 2004. "Policies for Urban Form and their Impact on Travel: The Netherlands Experience." *Urban Studies* 41(3): 579–603.

Slütter, Michel. 2012. "De Fiets Regeert in Amsterdam." *VogelvrijeFietser* March–April 2012. Amsterdam NL: Fietsberaad (Dutch Cycling Union).

Smart Mobility, Inc. 2010. "Moving Forward Together: Transportation Plan for the City of Burlington, Appendix 1: Technical Appendix." Mayor's Office, Burlington, Vermont.

Smith, Adam. 1776/1976. *An Inquiry into the Nature and Causes of the Wealth of Nations.* Chicago: University of Chicago Press.

Spinney, Justin. 2007. "Cycling the City: Non-Place and the Sensory Construction of Meaning in Mobile Practice." In *Cycling and Society,* edited by Dave Horton, Peter Cox, and Paul Rosen, 25–45. Burlington, VT: Ashgate Publishing.

Soja, Edward. 1992. "The Stimulus of a Little Confusion: A Contemporary Comparison of Amsterdam and Los Angeles." In *After Modernism: Global Restructuring and the Changing Boundaries of City Life,* edited by Michael P. Smith, 17–38. New Brunswick, NJ: Transaction Publishers.

Steg, Linda and Gifford, R. 2005. "Sustainable Transportation and Quality of Life." *Journal of Transport Geography* 13(1): 59–69.

Stein, Adam. 2006. "The Environmental Paradox of Bicycling Revisited." World Wide Website, accessed on January 12, 2012: http://www.terrapass.com/blog/posts/the-bicycling-p

Stein, Samuel. 2011. "Bike Lanes and Gentrification: New York City's Shades of Green." *Progressive Planning* 188: 34–37.

Stocking, George, ed. 1988. *Objects and Others: Essays on Museums and Material Culture.* Madison, WI: University of Wisconsin Press.

Stoekel, Allan. 2003. "Translator's Introduction." In *Need for the Bike,* by Paul Fournel, vii–xi. Lincoln, NE: University of Nebraska Press.

Suero, Diego. 2006. "La Bicicleta Como Medio de Transporte en la Ciudad de Bogotá." Unpublished manuscript, Universidad de los Andes, Bogotá, Colombia.

Tavernise, Sabrina. 2011. "A Population Changes, Uneasily." *New York Times,* July 17, 2011: http://www.nytimes.com/2011/07/18/us/18dc.html?pagewanted=all.

Thorns, David C. 2002. *The Transformation of Cities: Urban Theory and Urban Life.* New York: Palgrave Macmillan.

Troy, Austin. 2012. *The Very Hungry City: Urban Energy Efficiency and the Economic Fate of Cities.* New Haven, CT: Yale University Press.

Uitermark, Justus. 2009. "An *in memoriam* for the Just City of Amsterdam." *City* 13(2–3): 348–361.

Ulrich, Karl. 2006. "The Environmental Paradox of Bicycling." Working Paper: Department of Operations and Information Management, the Wharton School. University of Pennsylvania.

Underhill, Paco. 2004. *The Call of the Mall: The Geography of Shopping.* New York: Simon & Schuster.

Urry, John. 2007. *Mobilities.* Malden, MA: Polity.

Vannini, Phillip, ed. 2009. *Cultures of Alternative Mobilities: Routes Less Traveled.* Burlington, VT: Ashgate Publishing.

Vivanco, Luis. 2006. *Green Encounters: Shaping and Contesting Environmentalism in Rural Costa Rica.* New York: Berghahn Books.

—2010. "Hortense Powdermaker." In *Fifty Key Anthropologists,* edited by Robert Gordon, Andrew Lyons, and Harriet Lyons, 178–183. London: Routledge.

Wallace, Arturo. 2011. "Bogotá—Latin America's Biking Paradise." BBC News, July 20, 2011. World Wide Website accessed on July 2, 2012: http://www.bbc.co.uk/news/world-latin-america-14227373

Walljasper, Jay. 2012. "How cities can get drivers biking." *Yes!* Magazine, World Wide Website accessed on August 7, 2012: http://www.csmonitor.com/World/Making-a-difference/Change-Agent/2012/0807/How-cities-can-get-drivers-biking.

Wang, Rui. 2011. "Autos, Transit and Bicycles: Comparing the Costs in Large Chinese Cities." *Transport Policy* 18(1): 139–146.

Wilson, David Gordon. 2004. *Bicycling Science.* Cambridge, MA: MIT Press.

Wisniewski, Mary. 2011. "Chicago Mayor Rahm Emanuel Making Big Push for Bike Paths."
   Reuters. Sept. 24. 2011. World Wide Website accessed on 7/12/12: http://www.reuters.
   com/article/2011/09/24/us-chicago-bike-expansion-idUSTRE78N25520110924
Witte, Griff. 2004. "A Rough Ride for Schwinn Bicycle: As the World Economy Shifted, So Did
   the Fortunes of an American Classic." *Washington Post*, December 3, 2004, p. A01.
Wray, Harry. 2008. *Pedal Power: The Quiet Rise of the Bicycle in American Public Life*. Boulder, CO:
   Paradigm Publishers.
Xing, Y., S. L. Handy, and P. L. Mokhtarian, P. L. 2010. "Factors Associated with Proportions
   and Miles of Bicycling for Transportation and Recreation in Six Small U.S. cities."
   Transportation Research Part D: Transport and Environment 15: 73–81.

INDEX

Locators in *italic* refer to figures/illustrations

THE SOCIAL ISSUES
COLLECTION™